PSALM-HYMNS

Volumes One & Two

Psalms 1-72

Lyrics for Personal and Communal Reflection

Adapted by L. L. Larkins

Library of Congress Control Number:2019910374

Names: Larkins, L. L.
Title: Psalm-Hymns Volumes 1 & 2 Lyrics for Personal and Communal
Reflection, Psalms 1-72
Description: Littleton, Colorado : Capture Books, [2017] | Psalm-Hymns:
Lyrics for Personal and Communal Reflection | Words only. | Abridged.
Does not include bibliographical references and index.
Identifiers: ISBN-13: 978-1511856348 | ISBN-10: 1511856343
| ISBN 978-0-9971625-2-3 (ebook) 978-1-951084-02-8 (ebook)
Subjects: LCSH: Psalms (Music) | Hymns, English, American. | Bible--
Meditations. | Worship in the Bible | Drama Anthologies
Classification: LCC BS1424 .L37 2016 | LCC BS1424 (ebook) | DDC
223/.2052--dc23
MUS052000 Music; Lyrics DRA002000 | Drama; Anthologies; Multiple
Authors

Editors: Amy Hoppes, Crystal Schwartzkopf

Psalm lyrics

for personal performance

and communal reflection

CONTENTS

Dedication

To Jessica, Jamie, Sandy, Sophia, James, Elliott, Vanessa, Tommy, Phoebe, Charissa, Elijah, Christina and Joe:

Enoch, the father of Methuselah, and the great-grandfather of Noah, lived 365 years before he was taken by God from the earth without dying. The import of Enoch's life-walk with YAHWEH may seem less real to you than the myths of Grimm or the existence of Hobbits, Elves or Dwarfs. Stories of King David's mighty feats, though he was labeled the "Man After God's Own Heart," may seem more far gone than the tales of King Arthur of the Round Table. With these realities in mind, I dedicate this book to you children of my heart and family. Most of you in this generation have never known the memorable hymn tunes of my childhood. You, who may well believe the Psalms are just archaic relics of a nomad people and their violent god.

May you live long, productive lives and prosper.

Historical Uses

Most of the book of Psalms was written in the time of David and Solomon (c. 1010–970 BC). In all Christian, Messianic and Jewish traditions, the Psalms are utilized in corporate worship, referred to in training, and for celebrations or holy day traditions. Not since the days of the Puritans, however, has there been a comprehensive and accessible psalter for singing the Psalms. Originally, Psalms 1-119 comprised the Psalter, and it is thought that the Psalms of assents were added later.

The title of the Psalms is derived from the Greek translation, ψαλμοί *psalmoi*, meaning "instrumental music" and, by extension, "the words accompanying the music."

The Psalms are to be used for drama, recitals, school choirs, songs of praise, giving thanks, and prayers in worship. The Psalms are also used for purposes of teaching theology, devotional self-editing, history, and testimony. The Puritans used the Psalms in schools to teach children many things.

For students, philosophers, and gamers, the Psalms present some interesting puzzles to solve. We see through a dim glass, but what happens to the flesh, the spirit, and the soul after death? What does it mean for believers to testify of the safety and sanctuary of God in the midst of terrorism, disease, betrayal, false witnesses, and other afflictions? What is the difference between human law, human legal processes and God's law? Who is the King so often referred to in the Psalms? Why is God called by so many different names? How does salvation through Christ converge with obedience to God's law? What does loving one's neighbors mean when confronted with some Psalm petitions to eradicate one's enemies?

The book is an anthology, part one of 150 Psalms. I have indexed the Psalms below as to their purposed use and historical interpretation.

- True Torah Piety Psalms: Psalms 1, 2, and 150.
- Psalms 20, 23, and 72 are beautiful blessings for comfort.
- Psalms of Praise include: 8, 10, 18 (and thanks), 19, 21, 24, 29, 30 (with thanks), 36, 40 (with thanks), 41, 44, 45, 46, 47, 48, 50, 65 (with thanks), 66, 67, and 68.
- Pleading Psalms include: 3, 4, 5, 6, 7, 10, 13, 17, 22, 25, 26, 28, 31, 35, 43, 54, 64, 69, 70, and 71.
- Psalms of Lament can be divided into two kinds. The first is the individual laments, many written by David. These may include personal descriptions of misery, sickness, false accusations and a plea to the sanctuary for safety, confessions and complaints and other prayers. Others are communal Psalms of mourning and suffering due to the affliction of a small group or nation.

The Lament Psalms include: 3, 4, 5, 7, 17, 26, 27, 54, 55, 57, 63, and 69. Many of these contain pleas for divine judgment and are not limited to sacred ritualistic judgments or protections from the temple or sanctuary. Some however, can be understood as a prayer written to a judge or counselor who will then take the accusations and confessions, and render judgments—after which a group would seek to be reconciled again to live in harmony. A person's small group was how a person experienced meaning and religion.

Lament is an expression of examining one's soul in the light of God's love and righteousness. It is "the discipline of self-suspicion," a term coined by the Puritan minister, Thomas Manton, in England. On August 17, 1662, Manton preached his last sermon on Hebrews 12:1 just before The Act of Uniformity led to the "Great Ejection". Without bemoaning his own demise, he sweetly exhorted his congregation, "Watch over thyself with a holy self-suspicion, because thou hast sin within thee that doth easily beset thee; therefore *consider thy ways,* Psalm 119:59; *guard thy senses,* Job 33:1; but, above all, *keep thy heart,* Proverbs 4:23. Conscience must stand porter at the door, and examine what comes in and what goes out. Watch over the stratagems of Satan, and seducing motions of thy own heart."

- o Laments involving sickness, terror, disaster or misery include: 6, 13, 22, 28, 38, and 102.
- o Community Laments do not involve significant confession. They are: 44, 60, 74, 79, 80, 83, and 89.
- o Psalms which are considered in the Anthologies of the Exiled are: 25, 33, 34, 103, 111, 112, 119, and 145.
- Psalms of the Penitent are: 6, 32, 38, 51, 102, 130, and 143.
- Over 50 Psalms were written by David and are considered to be Psalms of royalty. Followers of Jesus began assessing the Messianic relationship of these Psalms early on as relating to Christ as the Liberating King. The most significant Messianic Psalms are: 2 and 22.
- The Sons of Korah were the faithful survivors of God's judgment against their dissenting father and cohorts who were swallowed when the ground opened up. They wrote Psalms of redemption, testimony, and praise, and Psalms of lament: 42, 43, 44, 45, 46, 47, 48, and 49.
- Teaching *Maskil* Psalms include: 52, 54, and 55. Each is considered to be an advocate of enlightenment. These Psalms can, and do, teach. Each and every Psalm is educational for righteousness.

- Psalms 11, 16, 23, 27, 46, 52, and 62 encourage us to rest in God's good sovereignty and might for safety when threatened.
- Psalms 12, 16, and 37 compares the LORD'S friendship to the oppression of traitors and deceivers.
- Psalms 14, 37, and 53 teaches the uselessness of fool's wisdom.
- Psalm 15 shows that the LORD will reject slanderers, gossips and defamers from heaven.
- Psalm 49 eloquently describes the error and foolishness of trusting in riches.

- Miktams are Psalm 16, 56, 57, 58, 59, and 60. These have a special instruction: to be performed with wind instruments or with just the voice which is a wind instrument itself. Miktam means "inscription" or "to cover." These Psalms may have to do with atonement, or because of the context of these Psalms, they may have indicated a whispered note, or, a secret note during a time of high alert or danger. They may have been a cover letter for a gift sent "under cover" i.e. Miktam (found only in books 1 & 2).

Although tunes have been chosen for each lyric, the style of how it may be sung may be as unique as each user. Try swing, or soul, or bluegrass styles besides the classic. Try dramatic readings, a cappella chorale, rock, or country. Just make a joyful noise to the LORD! Each Psalm is given space so that the musical user may add chord charts above phrases, references, musical indications, notes, or other thoughts.

~BOOK ONE~

(PSALMS 1–41)

PSALM 1

(A True Torah Piety Psalm)
Tune: THIS IS MY FATHER'S WORLD Trad. English melody;
adapt. by Franklin L. Sheppard

You'll be safe and on your way

To avoid the scoffer's play;

The counsel of ungodly minds

Leads only to dismay!

Oh, learn to love God's law!

Recall it day and night;

You'll prosper as you walk with God,

Enjoying what is right!

Like a little tree will thrive

Planted by the water's side,

In season it will yield its fruit,

How green its leaves abide!

See how these roots take hold,

Set against the roots that fail,

Swept up like chaff upon the wind,

The withered roots shall sail.

Defenseless in God's court,

The lawless cannot stand;

God's righteous hand will cast them out,

Their ruin close at hand.

The One, He is our God!

He cares for large and small.

The good intent, the provident,

He shall establish all.

Psalm 2

(A True Torah Piety Psalm, Messianic)
Tune: COME THOU ALMIGHTY KING
Orig. Italian Hymn, Felice de Giardini, (1769)

Why do the nations conspire?

Why are they spitting flames of fire?

Kings of this earth!

Rising against the LORD?

Mocking His Holy One,

"Come and throw down His rule.

Break off His chains."

From heaven's throne room, He laughs;

Sharpening the shock of His wrath,

Scoffing at wars,

Upsets their plotting scheme.

"I have installed My King

On Zion's holy hill,

See how He reigns!"

Sealing His own son as King:
"Now My anointed will reign!
 I am YAHWEH,
Acting as Father now,
Ask Me whatever, Son,
This, Your inheritance,
This world is won.

His rod of iron shall slay,
Dashing the plotters like clay.
Watch this you Kings,
Be wise and warned in this;
Serve God without remiss
Rulers who run to Him,
Keenly rejoice.

Kiss now His Son to escape,
Your stark demise on that day.
Never forget,
His wrath ignites your fate.
Run to him, don't delay.
Best that you hide in him,
Now and always.

PSALM 3

(A Psalm of David's lament when he fled from his son Absalom)
Tune: HE LEADETH ME, OH BLESSED THOUGHT
Orig."Golden Censer" William B. Bradbury (New York: 1864)

LORD, look! All those who cast their lot,

To topple me, how vast their plot!

The rumor grows and many say,

"God will not carry him today."

But You, Oh LORD, became my shield,

A buckler and a flag to wield;

My glory, and the One who lifts

My head to resolution, swift.

I'm calling out to God who wills,

He answers from His holy hill.

While I lie down, in sleep restored,

My confidence lies with the LORD.

I'm confident though thousands stride,

Assailing me on every side.

My LORD! Deliver, now arise!

My God, my ally, right on time.

LORD, strike them all, don't hesitate,

To break corruption's teeth, don't wait!

Your terms and venue, my rescue,

And God's deliverance shall be true.

Bless now Your people in Your will;

Anoint us LORD, Your servants fill.

LORD, bless us now, don't compromise;

For You, YAHWEH alone, are wise!

PSALM 4

(David's lament for evening worship with strings)
Tune: DAY BY DAY AND WITH EACH PASSING MOMENT
Blott en Dag, Oskar Ahnfelt (1872)

Father, answer me when I am calling;

God, You vindicate my humble choice.

You have freed me from my sore affliction;

So be gracious, LORD, and hear my voice.

How long will my honor be insulted?

Nobel men, persisting in a lie.

Lusting for the worthless and distorted.

Why won't they consider what is right?

Yes, the LORD has set apart the faithful,

For Himself, the LORD will hear my call.

Oh my soul, you tremble, but be careful;

Chill your anger, be direct and still.

On your bed, reflect on your condition;

Offer up your righteous sacrifice!

Trust the LORD, entrust to Him the outcome,

Trust the journey for He holds your life.

Many doubt and savor speculation:
"Who can show us any lasting good?"
Now, look on with favor, LORD, and save us,
Evidence of this residing joy.
My own heart knows deep resilient laughter,
Introduced by Your creative play.
This is joy much better than their feasting,
That their grain and harvest wines convey.

I will rest and I will dream reclining,
Peacefully, in sleep, I am restored;
For I know that You alone are faithful,
You're without exception, LORD of Lords.
This sweet safety isn't circumstantial,
For Your care is night and day supreme;
Making me, Your servant, live in safety,
You renew my life, increasing peace.

PSALM 5

(A Morning Lament, for the Refuge of the Righteous
for the Choir Director: with the flutes. A psalm of David.)
Tune: I KNOW WHO HOLDS TOMORROW
and I know Who Holds my Hand
Ira F. Stanphill 1950

Oh, consider my expression,

LORD; the pathos of my cry!

Pay attention to the passion,

Hear the sounds of life awry.

For I bring my tears to You, LORD;

You're my King and You're my God.

By the dawn, You'll hear my pleading;

Hear my case composed in sighs.

Now, I watch with expectation,

You are not a god who lies.

Putting all distortion from You,

With no cruelty in Your eyes.

Evil cannot dwell within You,
And the boastful cannot stand.
I'm refined within Your presence;
You despise an evil hand.
You destroy the lying spirits
And their treachery of voice;
LORD, abhor a man of bloodshed,
Oh, but LORD, let me rejoice!
See me entering the threshold
In Your house on heights above
Only by Your great compassion
And Your constancy of love.

Bowing down toward Your temple,

Now in reverential awe.

Oh LORD, lead me in Your lightness,

Higher ground will draw me up.

Hide me from my adversaries,

Will You open up Your way?

There are only crooked nothings,

Falling out of what they say.

Dank destruction lies within them,

And their throats are open graves.

With their tongues they twist and flatter;

God will punish them, I pray.

Let them fall by their devices;

Drive them out by their own schemes.

Of their many crimes, the greatest,

Is their hate for The Supreme.

Now, let all who take their refuge

In Your Love be ever sound.

Let them, sheltered by Your angels,

Shout in joy in sweet surround.

So may those whose consolation,

Sweet in Name, their love reveal;

Find our God, the LORD, protecting

By His blessing, by His seal.

PSALM 6

(One of David's Penitent Prayers for Mercy
with stringed instruments; for the ill)
Tune: GUIDE ME O, THOU GREAT REDEEMER!
(Bread of Heaven)
"Cwm Rhondda," John Hughes, (1907)

LORD, do not be rebuff me in Your anger;

Do not rout me in Your wrath!

Oh be gracious, LORD, for I am sickly,

Heal me, for my bones are lath!

My whole soul is terror-shaken

And, oh LORD, with You how long?

And, oh LORD with You, how long?

Turn, oh LORD! Now rescuing, restore me;

Save by loving faithfulness!

For there is no gratitude in passing

Who reminds the dead to praise?

I am weary from my groaning;

See, my bed is damp from tears!

See, my bed is damp from tears!

All these days have filled my eyes with sorrow

Swollen grief has swelled my eyes;

I grow old in opposition's railing.

Reprobates, they craft demise!

Leave me, all you evildoers,

For the LORD has heard my cry!

For the LORD has heard my cry!

Yes, the LORD has heard my quiet weeping;

He has heard my prayers for help!

I rejoice; the LORD'S response is holding!

All the reprobates shall melt

Shamed and shaken with His terror;

They will turn and be disgraced!

They will turn away, disgraced!

PSALM 7

(David's Lament and Frantic Prayer for Justice
Concerning the Words of Cush, a Benjaminite)
Tune: I KNOW NOT WHY GOD'S WONDROUS GRACE
(I Know Whom I Have Believed)
James McGranahan (1883)

Immortal God, I seek Your shield

For refuge in the cleft;

Hide me, oh, YAHWEH, from impending doom

As lion's prey, I live in dread.

    I am frightened that they will tear me up

    With many piercing teeth

    And none to rescue me!

    And I am frightened injustice will prevail

    I am frightened for the truth!

Immortal God, if I deserve this end,

You see injustice in my hands,

If I have harmed the one at peace with me

Or seized my adversary's stand,

    If without cause, my guilty acts are these,

    Oh, may an enemy, pursuing, seize on me;

    And trample my body to the ground,

    Leaving honor in the dust!

Rise up, oh, righteous LORD, in upright wrath;

Oh, arc and rain upon their fire!

Awake Your sentence of a just demise

Against the lion's sole desire;

    For You've ordered their end is just and sound.

    Oh, let the people see, assembled all around;

    Then sit high observing all who came,

    Take Your throne to judge the proud!

The LORD who judges all the nations' woes;

Will vindicate me by His Word,

Oh, LORD, according to my righteous cause

May my integrity be heard.

    Let the lions of evil see their end,

    Establish righteousness through those whom You

    Befriend.

    The One who examines thoughts and wills

    Is a high and healthy God!

My shield is of our God and righteous judge

Who saves the pure and upright heart,

A God who shows His anger every day

To vile and unrepenting hearts!

    God will sharpen His sword of justice now;

    He's strung His bow, it's taut, and piled weapons

    'round;

    His arrows, are tipped with fiery crowns:

    They will get what they deserve.

You see, the wicked one conceives deceit

And soon corruption will give birth.

The wicked dug a pit and cleaned it out

But toppled in the pit himself.

His troubles conceived for righteous feet

Came back on his own step, and violence fell on

him.

I thank God, the LORD of righteousness,

Singing YAHWEH's name Most High!

PSALM 8

(God's Wisdom and Creativity Exalted)
Tune: PRAISE TO THE LORD THE ALMIGHTY,
THE KING OF CREATION!
"Praxis Pietatis Melica," Lobe den Herren, Ander Theil des Erneuerten
Gesangbuch 1668

Oh LORD, our LORD, how majestic is

Your name the world-wide!

You spread Your glory above velvet

Evenings in night skies.

Mouths of the babes and nursing children dispute

All accusations against You.

When I consider Your heavens, the works

Of Your fingers,

The moon and the stars You have placed in

Their settings to swing there,

What are our minds? What are our souls that You care?

Why should Your kindness dispense here?

You, the Designer, made humans the
Minor to angels,
Crowned us with glory and honor and
Thus made us able,
Made us to rule over the stages of earth;
Handed this world to beginners:

All flocks and herds, and all
Crawling things roaming the wild,
Birds in the sky and all
Fish schooling through ocean isles
Oh, LORD, our LORD, certainly Your name is blessed!
Excellence showers Your conquests.

PSALM 9

(David's Celebration of God's Justice)
Tune: WHAT A FRIEND WE HAVE IN JESUS!
Orig. "When This Bloody War is Over" Charles C. Converse (1868)

I will thank The LORD immortal,

My whole heart declares His praise!

All Your work is splendid, always!

I will boast Your famous name;

I will sing Your highest honor

For my enemies' retreat;

They will trip and vanish quickly,

In Your presence, in Your heat.

LORD, You have upheld my standing,

Vindicated on Your throne

As a righteous judge rebuking

Nations for their wicked roles.

You erase their names forever

And eternal ruin comes.

How the enemy is broken;

And their cities in the sum!

See, the LORD established power

In His throne for evermore;

He established it for edicts

To the world, the rich and poor.

Executing proper judgments

With a Rightful Excellence;

Nations understand His fairness.

Standards of His elegance.

Yes, The LORD remains a refuge

For the pressed and heavy soul,

Those who know Your name and trust You,

Find You in their troubled world.

You do not desert the faithful,

Those who seek You, Ever-God.

Sing! This LORD, who dwells in Zion;

Shout the feats that He has done!

Righteous One Who keeps accounting

For the bloodshed of His own,

He remembers them and sorrows

For His persecuted ones.

LORD, be gracious to me also,

Lying low in deathly bands

Those who hate my righteous standing.

Lift me from their deathly hands.

Then, I shall declare Your praises;

I'll rejoice within Your walls;

Your salvation is my portion,

Gates of Zion are my halls.

Nations fall toward their gravestones

They made broad and careful nets;

But their secrets snagged their footing

And they tripped into their pits.

How the LORD reveals His Person!

With His executed plans,

Striking down the wicked trappers

By the work of their own hands!

Wicked souls return to Sheol

Rulers who dismiss our God.

Yet, You don't forget the humble;

You remember and applaud.

The great hope of the afflicted

Shall not perish in the end.

Raise Yourself above the mortals,

Judge the evil by Your hand!

Let the nations feel Your terror,

LORD; oh, let their regimen

See that nations' naked nobles

Are, in aspect, only men.

PSALM 10

(A Plea for Justice)
Tune: THE BLOOD WILL NEVER LOSE ITS POWER
Andraé Crouch (1969)

O LORD, You're standing so far away!

Why LORD,

O why do You hide from me?

For holiness won't mix with my poor trials,

But, the haughty hunt down the poor!

Oh, let their divisions trap them!

They brag on their greedy desires, and

Planning harm for others, cursing the Father,

Too proud and perverse for God.

But, LORD, Your punishment waits them out.

They think,

"The evil we do won't count."

And nothing of the trials of life will happen

For they say, "We're free of God!"

They act like the LORD is impotent!

They take God's forbearance for granted.

It makes no sense to see them win in everything!

While mocking poor innocents.

Their mouths are full of deceit and lies

Cursing

And threatening obscenities,

Their witnesses are evil tongues of poison.

How they spy and they ambush towns.

They're waiting to murder the innocents.

They're searching for helpless victims.

Like lions on the hunt, who pounce on weakness,

They drag them to bitter ends.

Defenseless victims are crushed beneath

Mighty men's

Deals and their corporate teeth.

The wicked come to think, "God isn't watching us!

He's closed His own eyes to see!"

Arise, LORD, to punish the reckless!

Oh, God, don't abandon the helpless!

Why do the wicked get away, despising?

They think, "God won't call us out!"

You see the trouble and grief they cause.

You take note

Of all their entourage.

You punish them, oh God, for the helpless trust You.

And orphans, You will regard.

Oh LORD, break the reach of the evil one!

Oh, chase down, destroy, his whole regimen!

Destroy the wicked souls and devil spirits.

For the LORD is the King of might!

Oh calm the friendless who trust in God!

You bring

Your justice for those in want;

And to an orphaned child, Your power nullifies

The menace who brought them down.

The godless of nations evaporate

From the lands God gave them to cultivate.

Oh, LORD, You know the hopes of Your dependents

Surely, You hear their cries today!

Psalm 11

(A Question of Refuge or flight)
Tune: JESUS, KEEP ME NEAR THE CROSS
W. Howard Doane (1869)

I have taken up my place in the LORD'S salvation.

With my refuge safely staged, what have I to question?

Why do you urge me fly, "Like a bird, to mountain?"

Why would fleeing to the hills be my best protection?

Should I risk the arrows poised with a skillful aiming?

Wicked pull their arrows taut, shooting for the gaming.

From the shade where they hide, they have wounded

Many!

Since you cannot bring good news, do not bring me any!

When foundations are destroyed, You will see us weighing

Whether any move we make could do much reclaiming.

On His throne, still the LORD lives in holy worship;

And His searching heavenly Eye makes a grand surveying.

He examines everyone, righteous and the wicked.

And He hates all those who love violent addiction.

He will rain burning coals, sulfur on their stations;

And a scorching wind will come bringing devastation.

For the LORD is strong and wise, upright in His doings;

Loving righteous follow-through, He loves righteous

Rulings.

One of these promises to the pure and upright

Is that they will see His face; glad in His approving.

PSALM 12

(For the Choir Director: According to *Sheminith*.

A Davidic Psalm of the LORD'S Friendship Versus the Oppression of
Deceivers)

Tune: OH I WANT TO KNOW YOU MORE

Steve Fry (1980)

Won't You help me, LORD, for those of faith have
disappeared;
Loyalty and truth have vanished from all human spheres.
Flattering and lies are now the means to ties that bind;
Those who split the truth have lost their access to Your
mind.

> May the LORD cut off deceit! All the slight of lips
> and mouths that flatter
> Vying for more power.
> Boasting far beyond the truth, masters of disguise,
> they're steering clear of
> All accountability. Oh,

> > How I need Your friendship, LORD!

"I am rising now to help You," promises the LORD.

"I have seen oppression and the groaning of the poor.

"I have witnessed Your affliction, waiting for your case;

"I will put the one who longs for truth in safety's place."

    See, His words are clear and pure! Pure like sterling
    silver from the fire,

    Seven times refined there.

    You, O LORD, will stand the guard, setting up Your
    Boundaries from deceivers

    Wandering and worthless, yet

        This generation worships them!

PSALM 13

(For the Choir Director:
The Howling Psalm of David, a Much-Tried Man)
Tune: BRETHREN, WE HAVE MET TO WORSHIP
"Holy Manna," William Moore, The Columbian Harmony (1825)

LORD, I'm asking, "How long, without exception,

Will You avoid and hesitate?

Did You forget me in my constant struggle

Pained with anguish every day?

How this sorrow drags me down low

Granting foes the upper hand!

Turn and answer, You're expected,

LORD my God, restore my stand!

If I die, in my upended status,

    Stop my adversaries' gloat;

Hear them chant, "Look there, we are crushing this!"

    Stop their triumph in their throat.

    Yes, I'm trusting in Your boundless

        Love: unfailing, faultless, free.

When You rescue, I will celebrate,

        Singing, "You are good to me!"

Psalm 14

(For the Choir Director: A Psalm of David Teaching the Uselessness of
Fool's Wisdom)
Tune: TAKE THE NAME OF JESUS WITH YOU
William Howard Doane (1860)
Alternate Tune: What a Friend We Have in Jesus

Fools delude themselves in thinking:

Look around you! There's no God.

They are useless and corrupted,

All their doings roughly shod;

    No, not one,

    Does any good!

    See, the LORD looks down from heaven.

    For He seeks a living wisdom:

    Whether anyone seeks Him.

Rogues will fool their very conscience,

Skew their hearts away from God.

They are useless and defective,

For their minds become corrupt.

No, not one,

Does any good!

Will the dreadful never learn?

They engorge on God's people,

They would never pray to Him.

Terror grips them in a moment,

These oppressors of the right

For Our God is moving by them

With His people at His side.

Wicked fools

Who oppress,

When their sense of right has died,

Breaching plans of the burdened;

But the LORD protects His child!

Who will come from Zion's Mountain

When the LORD restores His own?

Who will rescue Israel's promise,

All the people of the LORD?

> When the LORD

> The LORD restores,

> Then will Jacob shout with joy!

> And the people of Israel

> Will be merry with delight!

PSALM 15

(A Psalm of David.
Those Who Do Not Slander and Gossip May Enter)
Tune: STILL, STILL, STILL
Orig. Folk Tune (authorship unknown) from Salzburg

Who— may adore the LORD of Lords on high?

Who may enter into His Presence

On His holy hill of Defense?

Those— whose— feet lead on to blameless lives.

Do— what is right, speak truth to bring in light.

Never harm a neighbor in gossip,

And refuse to speak in slander.

Do— distain all those who bring demise.

Who— may— come to honor the King supreme?

Those who honor faithful mentors

Loving the LORD, in truth, will enter

Do— not— curse your friends in high esteem.

Who— may— come to worship the KING of Kings?

    Those who lend, not charging interest,

And not bribed to slight the innocent.

These— will— stand forever and serene.

PSALM 16

A Miktam "inscription" or "to cover."
Tune: I STAND AMAZED IN THE PRESENCE OF JESUS THE
NAZARENE (How Wonderful, How Marvelous)
Charles H. Gabriel, (Chicago, Illinois: 1905)

I come to You for refuge,

Oh, God, will You keep me safe?

I called the LORD, "My Master!"

And look, how much good I've gained!

All wonderful things come from You;

Every good and perfect gift!"

The godly ones in all the land

Are my heroes true and swift!

Difficulties and trouble,

Confusion will be the rod

For the backs who are leaning

Toward any other god.

I will never take part in any

Blood-sacrifices of their gods.

Nor— will I raise their idols' names;

You alone are God, my God.

You alone are my portion

I drink from a brimming cup

My boundaries lie in Assurance

Securing a pleasant lot!

Look, the land You gave me is pleasant land.

With horizons of surprise!

Sure inheritance makes me want to bless

You, my LORD, the One Who guides!

Even when I'm sleeping,

Woven in dreams at night,

My heart will me bring instruction.

You teach me to do what's right.

He will never leave! And He's always

Standing by to guard my place.

He is Faithful, God is for me.

It's no wonder I rejoice!

In my solace I praise You,

Safely, I rest my head;

Never will You leave me

Impoverished, among the dead.

And, You never leave Your dear Holy One

To the grave to rot away.

You will show to me life eternally,

Granting the joy of Your embrace.

Psalm 17

(A Plea and Lament)
Tune: HE GIVETH MORE GRACE WHEN THE BURDENS GROW
GREATER
twice orphaned Annie Johnson Flint (1910)

Oh, LORD, hear a plea for some justice and mercy;

Determine my cry, for I need Your defense.

Believe what I'm saying, in careful description;

Declare in the evidence, my innocence.

You've tested my thinking, examined my motives,

Scrutinized everything, found me upright.

In night, in the shadows, I come to You quickly,

Determined to say nothing wrong in my plight.

In following You, the commandments You gave us

Have kept me from trailing with the cruel and corrupt.

My steps have been faithful to stay on Your pathway;

I'm not indecisive, for You are enough.

I know You will answer because You will listen.

Bend down to my whisper, oh, God, hear my prayer!

Oh, show me Your unfailing love in Your mercies!

You exercise power, a refuge from fear.

O cover and keep me the apple of Your eye!

Hide me, a nestling, beneath Your strong wing.

Protect me and keep me from the wicked attackers,

Murderous enemies, slanderous stings.

For those without pity, are tracking, surrounding,

Listen to what they have boasted to do!

Watching like lions for chances to throw me,

Eager to ambush! I need Your rescue.

Ascending against them, oh, LORD! Rise above them!

Bring them to fall on their knees by Your sword!

Rescue me now with Your powerful holding;

Your wonderful hand, LORD, destroys their reward!

Remember Your children, the people You treasure,

And satisfy hunger 'til they want no more;

Leaving this legacy for their descendants:

The righteous shall see face to face You are LORD.

PSALM 18

(For the Choir Director: Praising God's Powerful Authority of Miracles A psalm of David, the servant of the LORD. He sang this song to the LORD on the day the LORD rescued him from his enemies, from Saul.)
Tune: VICTORY IN JESUS (I HEARD AND OLD, OLD STORY)
Eugene Monroe Bartlett Senior (1939)

I love You, LORD; my vigor!

You're my Fortress, and my Savior!

My solid God is solid Rock.

He shields me all my days.

He is my strong connection

and the power of protection,

And safe within His welfare,

I name Him the One to praise!

    Though ropes ensnared my shoulders;

    Though a flood of waste swept over!

    Though roots of death were twining round

    To choke my breath and air.

    I then began to holler out

    To the LORD who lives in heaven,

    Oh, I prayed to my God,

    And He heard every prayer!

The earth began to tremble;

And mountains shook down under;

His wrath moved the stony earth,

And a shroud of smoke poured out!

His mouth and nose shot fierce flames,

And glowing coals blazed from Him.

He parted heavens' watching crowds

And stepped down on black clouds.

    Oh, mounted on a mighty

    Angelic being He flew here,

    And soared out on pinions

    Of winds in stealth of dark.

    And veiling His approaching

    Were stormy clouds rebuffing.

    For they were a shield for

    The brilliance of His arc.

The clouds were raining lightning,

The hail in thunder sounding,

The LORD in heaven thundered;

The voice of the Most High!

And, suddenly with arrows

He scattered all the fallow;

The lightning bolts were flashing,

And obliged, they turned to sighs!

O LORD, upon Your order,

The blasting of Your roaring,

The ocean waves were parted,

I saw the earth laid bare!

And then He reached from heaven

And rescued me from drowning,

Oh, wonder of wonders!

He raised me out of there.

He rescued me from enemies

Too full of hate and muscle

Attacking me when I was down,

In trouble, feeling weak.

But there the LORD supported,

And He led me to some safety;

He rescued me for nothing more

Than He delights in me!

    The LORD rewards my choices,

    For doing right, rejoices;

    He kept me for my innocence,

    And brought me to my knees.

    I haven't turned from my God

    To follow after cheap frauds.

    See, clean hands are blameless,

    For I keep His decrees.

To the faithful You prove Faithful;

To the upright You are Upright.

To the pure You show Your purity,

But hide from the perverse.

To the crooked You show shrewdness.

For You rescue humble spirits,

But You humiliate the proud,

and shine around me first.

My LORD and God lights darkness!

His strength in me is endless.

And with His might an army

Is crushed like dust and spewed.

With God beneath supporting,

I scale the wall, reporting.

Oh, God's way is perfect.

His promises prove true.

For who is God except Him?

The LORD is our protection!

To all who look on Him for help,

Our God is solid rock.

Can anyone supplant Him?

He delegates and strengthens,

He makes my way a perfect path,

My feet like hind's feet walk.

    Surefooted as a deer on

    High mountain tops He makes me,

    He's training my battle hands

    With skill and flection sure.

    My arm is strong in drawing

    A bronze bow for aiming.

    Your right hand supports me,

    My salvation and shield!

You came to help me, aiding,

Your power came, invading,

On bended knee, You stretched me

And made my pathway broad,

You kept my feet from slipping,

I chased my foe and caught him;

I didn't stop 'til they were out.

I conquered with Your rod!

    For You have armed and saddled,

    You strengthened me for battle;

    I know LORD, You subdued

    My enemies by fleet.

    My foot went on their necks,

    And You granted them as subjects.

    My foes are destroyed now,

    And that was their defeat.

They called for help, but no one came

To rescue them or help them.

They even cried out to the LORD,

But He refused to move.

I pounded them so finely,

Dust in the wind, benignly,

I swept them to the gutter

Like so little dirt removed.

    This victory You granted

    Over all my sore and slanted,

    Appointed me the ruler

    Of the nations over all;

    And people I don't follow,

    Don't recognize, they serve me!

    As soon as they hear of

    My feats, they yield with pall;

The foreign nations cringe now

Before me, losing courage

And trembling, they're coming

From holdings now disgraced.

The LORD is well and healthy!

Praise to my Rock of plenty!

Oh, God of my salvation

Come and take Your lofty place!

    He is the God of vengeance

    Repaying those who harm me;

    Subduing nations under me

    And thwarts my enemies.

    My safety is beyond them;

    You save me from their violence.

    For this, LORD, I praise You,

    My King of Victory!

I'm singing praises to You, Your name will ring forever!

You granted me great victories as to Your chosen king;

To David and descendants, forever Your anointed!

Your love is unfailing, and victory You bring.

PSALM 19

Tune: ALL HAIL THE POWER OF JESUS' NAME
"Coronation Tune," Oliver Holden (1793)

The heavens shout God's handiwork,

    The skies proclaiming, shine!

    Like windows they reveal His light;

    Each day and night, they remind.

They have no speech, they use no words;

    But in their silence, they sign.

This mystery, like a bridegroom's love,

    Brings ardor in its zeal;

    Each day our dawning sun overcomes,

    Each night His knowledge reveals!

The sun was hung, in arc, by God

    For light to warm around the world.

His perfect Law brings drink to dry,

Refreshing every soul.

His Word will build the simple mind

To lean on Statutes in whole.

His every precept proves Him right

And all who listen find delight.

The LORD's Commands are radiant,

They bring us sight for life.

To fear the LORD is pure and right

He gives His guiding advice!

For His Decrees are proven firm,

And every one is found upright.

This golden honey from the comb,

Is caveat for life;

In keeping testimonies sure

We follow what they comprise.

For those who test Him prove no flaw,

His wonders they cannot define.

Oh, LORD, forgive my hidden faults.

    Save me from willful sins;

    Let no omission rule my life;

    I'm trusting in Your defense!

Untainted by the great deceits

    Let all my day be innocent.

May all recitals of my mouth

    Be pleasing offerings

    And be delightful in Your sight,

    My Bedrock, stable and deep;

May all my thinking bring You praise

    In my Redeemer's famous Name!

PSALM 20

(Blessing for Battle)
Tune: IN TIMES LIKE THESE
Ruth Caye Jones - Mother Jones (1943)

In troubled days, may God protect you.

In troubled days, may YAHWEH keep you!

And, may He send you heaven's help

The centered-strength that holds His home in Zion.

    May He recall your heart's lament.

    May He accept your humble tent.

    May He fulfill your prayers today

    And grant your heart's desire in full array.

May Jacob's God fulfill your purpose.

Oh, let our shout be joyful verses!

We lift our banner in God's name.

May YAHWEH fill all your requests today.

    I know the LORD gives victor's might

    To bless His Son, He answers sighs.

    From holy heaven, His right hand sweeps

    All mighty victories in His gripping feat.

Some people boast of wheels and leather,

While others boast strategic measures,

But we will raise our banner high,

Our God is YAHWEH!– He's our light.

 Their speed of arms collapsing, falls,

 But we rise up, stand firm to all.

 LORD, save the King, bring victory!

 Oh, bring Your answer on the day we call.

Psalm 21

(For The Choir Director. A Davidic Psalm On The King's Victory)
Tune: I LOVE TO TELL THE STORY!
William G. Fischer (1869)

Your strength, oh LORD! Your strength, oh God!

The King is gloating in strength!

He bursts for joy in You, LORD,

In the victory You bring.

His grateful joy has boasted: You gave His heart's desire,

Salvation for His people, the victory acquired.

    You met the King with riches;

    With blessings and ambitions,

    And on His head You placed there

    a crown of purest gold.

He asked You for abundant life,

And how You've given Him more! —

His length of days forever,

His great and glorious stores;

You poured on these through victory; conferring majesty

And dressed Him in Your splendor, forever blessed in

peace.

> You cheer Him with Your essence;
>
> The faithful loving Presence,
>
> And trusting in the Most High,
>
> unshaken stands the King.

Your hand will seize and capture all

Who hate You and Your will.

And like a fiery furnace,

Will burn when You appear;

The LORD's engulfing fire devours in His wrath,

And You will wipe descendants off of the face of earth.

> Though they expanded evil,
>
> Their harmful plans will fail them,
>
> For when You aim Your billows,
>
> their faces turn to flee.

Now be exalted, LORD of Lords,

The people love Your strength;

And we will sing Your praises

Your might will bring us peace!

Oh, LORD, the King rejoices in how Your strong hand saves

And greatly He's exulting for His beloved's grace.

    You met the King with riches;

    With blessings and ambitions,

    And on His head You placed there

    a crown of purest gold.

PSALM 22

(Messianic Psalm, Foreshadowing the Crucifixion)
Tune: A MIGHTY FORTRESS IS OUR GOD
Martin Luther, (1529)

My God, my God, don't fail me now!

Why vanish in my miserable grief?

My anguished cries are day and night,

Yet, You decline to save me!

The Holy One is crowned;

It's You all people praise.

In You, ancestors hoped

And trusted You to save.

They cried and were not put to shame.

But I am scorned by all around.

A worm to mock and not a man,

Contemptibly I crawl the ground.

Their insults fling, they make their plan.

"He trusts in God," they say,

"So let his LORD, YAHWEH

Deliver Him today!"

Derision is their tool.

Oh, don't forsake me, don't be late.

You caught me from my mother's womb;

I learned by faith to trust in You.

Now many bulls surround their prey;

And lions hotly here pursue.

They open wide their teeth.

I feel their tearing snare

I'm shattered like a pot

And water drains from fear.

Now all my bones are out of joint.

You lay me in the dust of death

My heart has melted, turned to wax,

My tongue clings dryly to the cleft;

Oh God, my God now don't hold back!

A pack of villains flay;

Preserve me from their sword!

They pierce my hands and feet.

My bones are on display;

How people stare and how they gloat.

They gamble for my garments, LORD,

dividing all my clothes for bid.

But even now LORD, don't be far

You are my strength; oh do come swift.

I shall declare Your name;

Now all who fear will praise!

With Jacob's heirs adore

This God who did not scorn

And would not hide His suffering son.

For by this theme God's praise is won

In great assemblies to be praised;

They know He shall fulfill His vows.

Accomplished, He will raise to save!

The poor will also eat,

And all the earth will turn

To see Him conquer death

He rules with deep concern.

The LORD is near, and never late.

With this He rules the nations.

The wealthy of the earth will feast

They worship just as all who go

Down to the dust before their king. —

All those who cannot keep

Their lives or legacies.

Posterity will serve

The LORD for all the earth

Each generation will be told.

The kingdom is the LORD's to keep.

A seed of truth shall serve him;

All shall be counted to the LORD

For generations to be born.

And they shall come to bless,

Declare His righteousness

To raise what was laid low

And everyone will know

That God alone has done this!

PSALM 23

Tune: AWAY IN A MANGER
Mueller, James R. Murray (1887)
Or IMMORTAL, INVISIBLE, GOD ONLY WISE
St. Denio (1839)
Or Cradle Song Away in a Manager
William J. Kirkpatrick

The LORD *is* my shepherd;

He meets every need;

He makes me lie down in

Green meadows for peace;

He leads me beside the

Still waters for drink.

And there He restores my soul;

There, He gives strength.

My shepherd leads over

The paths we must take

In love and in righteousness

For His name's sake.

Although we pass through

Vales of shadowy death,

I fear, there, no evil

No perishing breath.

For You are beside me;

Your rod and Your staff

Bring comfort to guide me

To rest and to laugh.

You spread me a feast

In the presence of foes;

Your oil anoints me,

My cup overflows.

My cup spills with plenty,

Restoring my soul.

And mercies will follow me;

Goodness will grow.

Through all of the days of my life

I will dwell

Forever, oh LORD, in

Your house to live well.

Psalm 24

(Hymn of Praise to God)
Tune: AT CAVALRY
(Years I spent in vanity and pride)
William R. Newell after a rebellious youth (1895)

All the fullness of the earth begun,

Land and spaciousness for everyone,

All of it including what may come:

It is the LORD's!

For He founded it upon the seas, drawing limits,

Drawing floods and springs.

Who shall come to Him, ascend His hill?

It is the LORD's!

Who shall stand within His holy place?

One, whose hands are clean and filled with grace;

One, whose heart is pure and does not

swear deceitfully;

One, who ran the race discarding pride,

Didn't lift a soul to vain demise;

He receives the blessing from the LORD,

adorned on high!

Righteousness is from the God who saves.

This, the generation of His grace,

They that seek Him, seek His holy face,

and Jacob sighs!

Lift your heads, O gates; and lift them high!

You with everlasting doors swing wide!

And the King of glory shall come in to visit them!

Who is this, the glorious King Who won?

He, the strong and mighty LORD Who comes,

This, the LORD of might in battle fights.

Lift high you gates!

While you're lifting up, your long-closed doors;

Greet the King of glory and adore.

"Who," you ask, "is such a splendid King?"

He is the LORD!

PSALM 25

(In the Anthology of the Exiled.)
Tune: HIS EYE IS ON THE SPARROW
(Why do I feel discouraged?)
Charles H. Gabriel (1905)

Forward to You, I'm lifting

Lifting my soul, O LORD,

Trusting You, O my Father,

Waiting in the unknown;

Oh, may my faith be supported,

Faith so preciously poured,

Let me not be ashamed, LORD—

Or God, by You, ignored;

Where's a trusting soul who is lacking great reward?

    I sing because You hold me, You are my

    Guaranty!

    Your eye is on the sparrow, and I know

    You're Watching me.

May Your betrayers falter,

They are without a cause;

May the corrupt be halted

While all the faithful watch.

Let my faith be commissioned!

Lead me bright as day,

As You are training and guiding,

I follow in Your way,

Live in Your decrees, LORD; You are One who saves!
(chorus)

You *are* my God and Savior;

I'll wait for You to bless.

Bring me Your tender mercies

And loving-kindnesses.

For, they are ancient and faithful.

Wipe away every sin,

Those of youth I've committed,

And all my transgressions;

Undeserving mercy! You see me through Your lens!

    I sing for You preserve me,

    You are my Guaranty!

    For Your eye is on the sparrow, and I know

    You're watching me.

Oh, LORD, You're good and upright;

Teaching us all Your ways,

And You will guide the humble,

Guide them through all their days,

Yes! The FATHER is gracious

Full of Mercy and Truth;

And all who treasure His edicts

Know tales of how He moves.

For His sake He pardons all my sins accrued!

Where is the soul who fears Him?

This is what God intends.

You'll make a proper living,

Prospering by His hand.

And descendants inherit

All the earth at their feet.

Yes! For this is the secret:

The LORD abides with these.

All who venerate Him, He will bring them peace.

> I sing because You keep me,
>
> You are my Guaranty!
>
> For Your eye is on the sparrow, and I know
>
> You're watching me.

His covenants, my promise.

Therefore my eyes *are* fixed

Looking toward the SAVIOR,

Watching redemption's mix.

So, turn to show off Your mercy!

Pluck my feet from the mesh.

Desolate and afflicted,

You know my great distress!

Look on this affliction; forgive my sinfulness.

Consider, LORD, You found me—

With enemies great and small;

Many distressed me cruelly,

Yet, You redeem Your Own!

Save my life, and deliver;

Let Israel not be ashamed,

Oh, may my honesty save me,

Integrity of name.

May cohesion serve me! I wait Your splendid fame.

>I sing for You preserve me,

>You are my Guaranty!

>For Your eye is on the sparrow, and I know

>You're watching me.

PSALM 26

(A Plea for Vindication and Lament)
Tune: THE LONGER I SERVE HIM,
THE SWEETER HE GROWS
Bill Gaither (1965)

Vindicate me, LORD of Heaven,

In my journey and life;

For my virtue was in trusting

In Your faithfulness helping me thrive.

So test me, and try me, examine my mind.

For Your love is faithful, LORD, always nearby,

I live by Your truth, with my whole heart I trust You,

Oh be there, exonerate, when I am tried.

I do not endorse the worthless

Or pretenders of saints.

Loathing crowds of evil doers,

I do not approve of deceitful complaints.

So test me, and try me, examine my mind.

For Your love is faithful, LORD, always nearby,

I live by Your truth, with my whole heart I trust You,

Oh be there to vindicate, when they ask why.

I have washed my hands in honor

'Round Your altar, O LORD,

Raising vocal, loud thanksgivings

Retelling how wonderful all Your works are!

　So test me, and try me, examine my mind.

　For Your love is faithful, LORD, always nearby,

　I live by Your truth, with my whole heart I trust You,

　Oh be there to liberate, when I am tried.

LORD, I love the house You dwell in,

Where Your glory resides.

Do not cast me off with schemers,

Or leave me behind with their bloodshed and bribes.

　So test me, and try me, examine my mind.

　For Your love is faithful, LORD, always nearby,

　I live by Your truth, with my whole heart I trust You,

　Oh be there to vindicate, when they ask why.

Since I live with sincere honor,

Buy my life with Your grace.

I stand on Your firm foundation,

Extolling the LORD in the court's crowded place.

PSALM 27

(A Lament of David)
Tune: IMMORTAL, INVISIBLE
Orig. St. Denio, Welsh melody, from Canaidau y Cyssegr,
by John Roberts (1839)
Or AWAY IN A MANAGER

The LORD is my Light and my constant Estate!
Then whom shall I fear when His Stronghold is safe?
Though evil advances against me for ill
To slander, devour me all will be well.

My rivals and enemies stumble and fall.
Though armies besiege me, I fear none at all;
Though warriors may shake down a valiant defense,
Then yes, God alone is my sheer confidence.

This one thing I seek and I ask from the LORD,
To hold my insurance for life at the Source
To gaze on His beauty to seek His embrace
For here in my trouble He will keep me safe.

Though hiding in shelters in His sacred tents
He sets me on high over enemy angst.
My head is exalted and here I will sing
In shouts to my Savior, in songs to my King.

Be merciful, hear me and answer my cry.
I speak to my heart, "Seek His face now or die;"
Your face, LORD, I seek. Do not hide it in rage,
Oh, don't turn or leave me, oh, Helper who saves!

And yes, though a father and mother take leave,
The LORD will receive me; to Him I will cleave.
Now, lead me in honesty, spite all my foes.
I wait for the LORD, oh take heart, He is close!

PSALM 28

(Prayer to My Strength)
Tune: I GO TO THE ROCK
(Where Can I turn when there's nobody else to listen?)
Dottie Rambo (1967)

LORD, I will call

To You, my Rock. Do not be silent!

If You ignore me,

Playing deaf to needed guidance,

Then I'll be just like

All the spirits going downward,

Down to the pit, a bottomless pit, So hear my cry!

    I go to the Rock, oh, won't You listen, (LORD),

    To the sound of my petition,

    With my hands uplifted, here, for what I need?

    When all around me are crooked souls,

    Don't haul me down to the pit with fools!

    When I cry for shelter, for Your holy shelter,

    I go to the Rock.

Seeing all those

Talking friendly with their neighbors

Keeping back burners

So hot with bad behavior!

Won't You repay them?

LORD! and tend to all their evil!

Here, I lament these hypocrites, Oh! Pay them back!

    I go to the Rock, oh, won't You listen, (LORD),

    To the sound of my strident petition,

    With my hands uplifting, here, for what I need?

    When all around me are crooked souls,

    Don't haul me down to the pit with fools!

    When I cry for shelter, for Your holy shelter,

    I go to the Rock.

Yes, there are those

Couldn't care less for the LORD'S favor,

What He has fashioned,

And finished as our Savior!

Now, He will tear down,

Those souls and not rebuild them.

May He be praised, the LORD be praised, He heard my cry!

    I go to the Rock, oh won't You listen, (LORD),

    To the sound of my petition,

    With my hands uplifting, here, for what I need?

    When all around me are crooked souls,

    Don't haul me down to the pit with fools!

    When I cry for shelter, for Your holy shelter,

    I go to the Rock.

The LORD is my Strength!

He's my Shield; oh how I trust Him!

And, I am helped up,

That's why my heart rejoices!

And I extol Him

With my song forever ringing;

God is the Stronghold for all His people; He is our Strength!

     I go to the Rock, oh, won't You listen,

     To the sound of my strident petition,

     With my hands uplifting, here, for what I need?

     When all around me are crooked souls,

     Don't haul me down to the pit with fools!

     When I cry for shelter, for Your holy shelter,

     I go to the Rock.

This, His Anointed,

Is my Stronghold of Salvation,

Saving His people,

LORD! We are Your possession!

Shepherd us onward!

And, carry us forever!

When I need a helper, when I need help, I go to the Rock.

    I go to the Rock, oh won't You listen,

    To the sound of my strident petition,

    With my hands uplifting, here, for what I need?

    When all around me are crooked souls,

    Don't haul me down to the pit with fools!

    When I cry for shelter, for Your holy shelter,

    I go to the Rock.

PSALM 29

(A ROYAL PSALM, A PRAISE HYMN FOR THE VOICE OF THE LORD)
Tune: ANGELS WE HAVE HEARD ON HIGH
Orig. Languedoc, France. Unknown author. Public Domain.

All you angels, heavenly beings,

Sons of heroes, sons of kings:

To the LORD on high ascribe,

Glory due His name on high!

    Glo~~~ria

    Strong in full resplendence!

    Glo~~~ria

    In His Holy Presence!

YAHWEH's voice is far revered,

High above the atmosphere.

God in glory sends His voice

Decibels are thunderous!

    Glo~~~ria

    Strong in full resplendence!

    Glo~~~ria

    In His Holy Presence!

The voice of the LORD will shower

In its splendor, in its power

Breaking trees of Lebanon,

Cedars scattered in a song!

    Glo~~~ria

    Strong in full resplendence!

    Glo~~~ria

    In His Holy Presence!

Lebanon skips like a calf,

And Mount Hermon, too, will laugh.

Young and wild Sirion,

Soon will laugh for old is young.

    Glo~~~ria

    Strong in full resplendence!

    Glo~~~ria

    In His Holy Presence!

Do you hear God's flashing voice?

It will shake the wilderness,

Flames of fire when it pours,

When His voice on Kadesh roars!

    Glo~~~ria

    Strong in full resplendence!

    Glo~~~ria

    In His Holy Presence!

The voice of the LORD shall make

Deer give birth and live oaks shake.

It will strip the woodlands bare.

It will make the forest ache.

    Glo~~~ria

    Strong in full resplendence!

    Glo~~~ria

    In His Holy Presence!

In His temple, hear them cry,

"Glory! Adoni, on high!"

At the flood the LORD was King,

When the flood rose, He supplied.

    Glo~~~ria

    Strong in full resplendence!

    Glo~~~ria

    In His Holy Presence!

Adonai, enthroned in peace,

Giving all His people strength;

King forever, He is wise,

Blessing them with peaceful ties.

    Glo~~~ria

    Strong in full resplendence!

    Glo~~~ria

    In His Holy Presence!

PSALM 30

(A Dedication. Morning Psalm of Thanksgiving,
A Psalm of David for the Dedication of the Temple)
Tune: CROWN HIM WITH MANY CROWNS
"Diademata," George J. Elvey, (1868)

I will exalt You, LORD,

You raised me from the depths;

You would not let my rivals gloat

In all You did direct.

I called on You for help,

Then LORD, You saved and healed.

You spared me from the pit of hell

And raised me from the dead.

Sing! Sing with me in faith

The praises of the LORD.

Oh, praising His glorious name on high,

All faithful ones restored.

His anger quickly blasts,

And yet His favor comes

Though weeping lingers in the night,

Yet joy comes with the dawn.

Oh, when I felt secure,

That shelter would not end,

That's when I learned Your favor comes

As God made me stand firm.

My royal mountain stood

Until You hid Your face,

Then in dismay I called to You,

In pity, You showed grace.

"What would You gain if I

Were silenced in the pit?

Would dust rise up to praise Your name,

Or bandits silence it?

Oh, LORD, become my help!

Your mercy cover me!

You turned my wailing into dance;

In You, I found reprieve."

Now in my soul I sing

Your attributes and shout.

Oh LORD my God, I honor You

With strength and will poured out.

Forevermore I'll sing,

Of God, whose covering,

Transformed my wailing into dance

And made my spirit breathe.

PSALM 31

(A Plea for Protection from Disgrace. For the Choir Director)
Tune: WHEN I CAN READ MY TITLE CLEAR TO MANSIONS IN THE SKY
"Pisgah," Scottish tune, arr. by Joseph C. Lowry in
"The Kentucky Harmony," by Ananias Davisson, 2nd Ed., 1817;
harmonized by Austin C. Lovelace in The Book of Hymns (Nashville,
Tennessee: 1966)

I seek to find in You, O LORD,

A refuge from disgrace.

Oh, listen close and rescue quick all by

Your righteousness.

All by Your righteousness,

All by Your righteousness,

Be a mountain fortress, listen close,

All by Your righteousness.

Since Your name is a mountain fortress,

You can lead and guide me home.

Will You free me from the secret nets,

And bring me back to You?

Oh, bring me back to my Redeemer,

Bring me to the God of truth.

Into Your hand I entrust my soul, oh,

Bring me back to You!

I loathe all those who are devoted

To their worthless idols.

I trust in You and Your faithful love,

So gladly I rejoice.

So gladly I rejoice, so gladly I rejoice!

For when You noticed all my trials,

How gladly I rejoiced!

You didn't hand me to the enemy,

Set my feet in spacious place!

Haven't handed me to the enemy.

So gladly I rejoice.

You've set my feet in a spacious place,

LORD, oh won't You be more gracious now

In my distress and tears?

In my distress and weary tears,

In my distress and weary tears,

From my angry tears

My angry sorrow, fragile mortal griefs consume my life!

It was my sinfulness that caused

My years on earth to shorten in waste.

My bones are dry, they ridicule, and

Mock me everyone.

They mock me everyone, in gossip,

Mock me everyone!

My post are broken and forgot, they mock me everyone!

When they conspired against my life,

I trusted in my LORD God.

My course of life lies in Your hand,

My God, deliver me!

My God, deliver me, my God deliver me!

Show favor to Your servant, LORD, and

Save me by Your love.

And when I call, LORD, do not let me

Be disgraced in sore contempt.

Oh, silence it, oh let the wicked

Be themselves brought low.

Be themselves brought low.

Be themselves brought low!

May lying lips be silenced, LORD, will all the arrogant.

How great is Your storehouse of goodness

Kept for those who hide in You!

You accomplish good in the sight of all

For those who hide in You.

For those concealed in Your protection,

Those who hide in You,

Your presence is a shelter~stone from

Schemes of quarrelsome tongues.

Extol the LORD for He has proven

Wonderful and faithful!

For in a city under siege, I thought You could not see.

I thought, oh LORD, You could not see.

I thought You could not see!

I doubted in alarm, but LORD,

You brought me liberty!

So love the LORD, and hope in Him, for

He protects the loyal ones.

But He repays the arrogant, so be strong,

Not proud, be brave.

Be strong, not proud, be brave;

Be strong, not proud, be brave;

Take courage You of little faith.

The LORD, Himself, will save.

PSALM 32

(Penitent's Psalm)
Tune: ALL GLORY LAUD AND HONOR
"St. Theodulph, Melchior Teschner," "in Ein andächtiges Gebet"
(Leipzig, Germany: 1615)

The one whose sin is covered,

Transgressions written off,

The same is counted righteous,

Adopted and faultless!

When I kept silent in my sin,

these bones grew thin and old

I groaned all day from failing health for

Your hand took ahold.

This drought of summer lifted

When I came out to You;

I saw there was no hiding,

And changed my lies to truth.

Yes, You forgave the lot of all that

blackness in my soul!

I'm breathless! You removed my bleak

iniquity in whole!

So this is why the godly

All pray to You alone;

For certainly they find You;

I timely found Your throne!

And certainly in sweeping floods their

end shall not be grim.

You *are* my hiding place, Oh LORD;

from trouble and from him.

You shall preserve my spirit

With sweet deliverance,

You shall surround my soul with

A singing reverence.

You tell me, "I will teach you in the

Way that you should go;

And I will guide you with My eye;

Instruct you there below."

Don't be a bitter mustang

Don't be a stubborn mule,

Aside from bit and bridle

These banal beasts are dull.

They will not saddle up to you;

don't be that way with Me.

You've seen how many sorrows fall on

Hostile wayward beings."

Now should you trust the LORD HIGH,

With focused harmony,

Devotion shall surround you.

And continuity.

So shout for joy, you right in heart!

And all together praise!

There is no higher verdict than what

ADONAI will raise!

QUESTA IMMAGINE DI DANTE
SOTTRATTA ALLE OFFESE NEMICHE
QUI ANCORA ATTESTI
OLTRE L'AVVERSO DESTINO
L'INDOMITA FEDE DELLA GENTE ISTRIANA
NEL PROPRIO DIRITTO
COME UN DÌ A POLA PRESSO DEL CARNARO
CHE ITALIA CHIUDE E SUOI TERMINI BAGNA

PSALM 33

(In the Anthology of the Exiled.
Praise To The Trustworthy LORD)
Tune: I'LL FLY AWAY (SOME GLAD MORNING)
Eugene Monroe Bartlett Senior (1930)

May the godly sing aloud with joy

For YAHWEH is LORD;

How this gladness fits them like a crown,

In beautiful awe!

Beautiful awe will praise Him,

Fitting and pure!

Praise the LORD with melodies on strings;

Oh, sing His allure!

Sing new praises to the truest LORD,

And skillfully play!

Sing with joy for all His Word is worth;

Words, true as day!

Everything our LORD does is

Valiant and just!

And He loves the mirror in trusting hearts

With unfailing love!

God poured out His everlasting love
To all of the earth.
He spoke just a word, and by His breath,
The heavens were birthed.
All heaven's stars were born and
Skies were contained,
He locked oceans into reservoirs
Of seas He ordained.

Let the whole world fear the LORD of all, and
Tremble in awe.
When He spoke, the earth began to whirl,
Yes, this is our LORD!
We see the Master thwarting
National schemes
See His future Principal confirmed,
And His will esteemed.

Joy awaits a nation for expressing,

"God is the LORD."

His sweet legacy is for His chosen,

Gain His reward!

Searching around from heaven's

Throne, God observes;

Watching over every living race,

He watches the earth.

God has fashioned every motivation;

He understands.

Everything we do is comprehended as

By His hand.

The best equipped of armies

Can't save a king,

And a soldier will not find escape

By well-armored strength.

Horses cannot bring the victory

For all of their might.

YAHWEH saves all those who stand in awe

Of Him in the fight!

We can rely on His love,

Never undone,

Caring, keeping faithful through a famine's

Lean seasons.

We put all our hope in Adonai for

He is our shield!

His name means the Master of our Help, when

Hearts are revealed.

We can be merry for His

Name is our Trust!

Let Your loving kindness now embrace

With unfailing love!

PSALM 34

(In the Anthology of the Exiled.
In David's exuberance, He wrote these Words.)
Tune: HOLY, HOLY, HOLY
"Nicaea," John B. Dykes (1861)

I will bless the LORD in every situation!

Bless Him in complexity

and critical affairs!

Boasting Him, and praising, fills my conversation.

My soul shall make glad, humble hearts repair.

Come, exalt the LORD'S name, magnify Him, praising.

Come with me, and let us shout

the wonders of His name!

I have sought the LORD, and hearing, He delivered!

All of my fears fled, avoided when He came.

Radiant from looking on the LORD of glory,

No expression on their face of

Shame or shadow there.

This poor person cried out to the LORD who heard him,

Creating safety, saved him from despair!

Angels of the LORD encamp about and cover

All who fear the LORD of Hosts

Who does deliver them!

Come with me and taste, oh, see how good the LORD is!

Each one will prosper, all *who* trust in Him!

Oh, defer your fears to this the LORD, Almighty!

Listen, Saints, there *is* no want

for those who fear my King.

Young and hungry lions lacking skill are needy;

Yet those who seek Him lack for no good *thing!*

Come and hear, you children, anyone who loves life;

I will teach you awesome things

about the LORD'S long arm!

Do you long for full life, *many* days, of good life?

Don't be deceitful, keep your lips from harm.

Now withdraw from evil, deviate to do good;

Seek His peace, pursue His peace,

For God is watching you.

How His ears are open to the righteous crying,

His face opposes those in evil queues.

Atlases erase them, all the earth forgets them.

Yet, to hear the *righteous* cry,

The LORD is not aloof!

He is near to all who have a broken spirit,

Seeing this meekness, moves His chariot's hooves.

Many troubles a just and honest lifestyle,

Yet the LORD will save the righteous soul

From all their groans.

Guarding all His bones; Not one of them is broken.

Evil shall slay the wicked on its own.

Haters of the righteous are condemned as aimless,

And the LORD redeems the souls

of all His servants brave.

None of those who trust Him

shall be doomed or sentenced.

He will deliver! Trust the LORD to save!

PSALM 35

(A Nishmat –breath– of David)
Tune: GOD REST YE MERRY GENTLEMEN
Orig. English Roud Folk Song (1833)

Contend, O LORD,

Contend with those

Who fight and strive with me!

In competition, take my part,

Take up a shield, I plea!

Arise and bring Your armor here,

Arise and come for aid.

Oh, brandish Your javelin and spear,

and make a play!

Pressing in pursuit, we shout Your saving grace!

May those who seek

To end my life

Be quit and put to shame;

May those who plot my ruining

Be turned back in dismay;

Their weight be insignificant

And light as chaff on wind.

May the Almighty be in hot pursuit,

in angel's breath;

May their path be dark in slippery torment.

Since, without cause,

They hid their nets

For me and dug a pit,

May ruin overtake them by

Surprise of nets they hid.

And when they fall into their pit

In joy my soul will leap

To the LORD of Salvation, exclaiming,

I will sing,

"Who is like our LORD and Leader, who competes?

You rescue poor

From those who are

Too strong and fully armed;

You rescue poor and needy from

The robbers who do harm."

When ruthless witnesses come forth

To question me on things

Having nothing to do with me, repaying

bad for good,

They abandon me as lost, and in my grief!

I fasted humble

Prayers for them when

Their loved one grew ill.

And, when my prayers returned to me

Unanswered, I was still.

I mourned as for my own dear friend,

And bowed in weeping grief

As bereaved for my brother or my mother,

was my grief.

Why then, when I stumbled, they appeared in glee?

Assailants circled,

All against

in opposition spoke,

Without my knowledge, slandered me;

Maliciously, they joked

Like godless creatures gnashing teeth,

Without a cause, they breathe;

O how long will You mildly look on their

raving words?

O Lord, lift me from these lions' dreadful claws!

I will give thanks

To You, O Lord,

In great community;

Among the masses I will praise You.

Don't let enemies

Come gloat or hate maliciously

On me without a cause,

Winking eyes, speaking peace but playing games

for their increase,

Making accusations in their gloating sprees.

They point their hand

Against the quiet ones

Who live on land.

They sneer at me and say, "Aha!

Our witnesses will stand."

LORD, have You seen this? Are You mute?

Oh, don't go far abroad!

Now, awake! to contend for me and rise to

my defense!

Vindicate me in Your righteousness, my God.

May all who gloat

In my distress

Be bowed and put to shame;

May those who lord it over me

Wear rags and bitter chains.

May those delighting in my vindication

shout for joy

And in gladness say, "Be exalted, LORD, for

You delight

In the comforts of Your servant, You are right!"

PSALM 36

(A Hymn of Incredulous Joy for God's Amazing Love)
Tune: BENEATH THE CROSS OF JESUS
"St. Christopher," Frederick C. Maker (1881)

Sin whispers to the wicked

In caverns of their hearts.

They have no fear of God at all,

Or see the ruin they are.

In blind conceit,

They cannot see how crookedly they speak.

In every aim deceitful plots,

With cursing thoughts they think.

Sin whispers to the wicked,

Perverting what is wise.

Refusing acts to help with good,

They lie awake at night.

They hatch the plots that bring on fights,

Their acts are never good.

They never make attempts to turn

From evil back to God.

Your Love, oh, LORD, unfailing,

Is vast as heaven's breadth!

Your Faithfulness, pervades the skies,

Like endless high croisettes,

Your Righteousness is like the mass of

Mighty mountains' girth,

Your Justice, like the ocean depths,

Holds mysteries of earth!

You care alike for people

And animals, oh LORD.

How precious is Your love, O God!

Unfailing its regard.

All humans find their shelter in

The shadow of Your wings.

You feed them from the plenty of

Your house, and let them drink.

You faithfully feed clouds which

Then burst into Your streams.

Your river of delights is found

In light by which we see.

For You, oh LORD, uniquely form

The fountain of all life,

Pour out Your love like rivers flow

On those who love Your heights.

Give justice to the honest

Of heart, the true, sincere.

Don't let the proud run over me

Or trample me in fear.

Don't let the wicked take my stand,

Now Look! They trip and fall.

They're thrown to pits of humble ground

To never rise at all!

PSALM 37

(A Teaching Psalm)

Tune: LEANING ON THE EVERLASTING ARMS
Anthony J. Showalter (1924)
To be sung antiphonally by two choruses:

Don't you fret about, don't you envy those

Sinful people who enjoy their wrongs.

Like the grasses wilt, like the flower fades,

They are singing but a last swan song.

Trust Him, Trust Him!

Find delight and keep on doing good.

Indulge in the LORD,

You'll be fine in living as you should.

He will keep you safe, when you cultivate

In the land He helped you to acquire.

He will help you thrive, still your soul and wait,

He will give you what your heart desires.

Dedicate everything,

All you do and all you are to God.

Rest in Him, wait for Him;

Don't be anxious at a thriving fraud.

How your purity shines as bright as dawn,

How the justice of your cause shall shine!

He will fashion you like the brightest sun.

Keep on doing good and you'll be fine.

Trust Him, Trust Him,

Find your joy and keep on doing good.

Take delight in the LORD,

You'll be fine in living as you should.

What's that angry tear? Turn your rage from here.

Don't lose heart or let your temper flare.

It will lead away, lead to harm and fear

Trust in God, and work the land He gave.

Obstinate rebels waste;

Though you look for them you'll see a void.

Look now! Look now,

God has cut them off, they are destroyed.

Those who trust in Him shall possess the land.

Though they're lowly, they will reap rewards!

They will live in peace and prosperity

Though the wicked draw and grasped for more.

Faithless mobs plot against
Children who obey the LORD;
He laughs, He laughs!
Their calamity is soon deployed.

Wicked draw their knives, string their bows to fight,

Planning how to slay the poor in health,

In their lust to kill pure and righteous lives,

Their own swords will break and wound themselves.

He saves! He saves!

He's a shelter in the bitter storm.

Look to honest souls,

You'll discover peace and rich reward.

Being near to God, though with little else,

Bests the wicked in their richest hour.

While the LORD protects, lifts His own to rest

Vile arms will break and curses groan.

He protects, He directs

Faithful leaders in the steps they take.

He delights day and night

In the factors of the lives they make.

Day by day the LORD feeds His faithful ones,

They inherit everlasting life.

When the times are hard He won't disregard;

Where there's famine they'll be satisfied.

The LORD's enemies

Are like flowers in a field that die

The depraved disappear.

Up like smoke they vanish with a cry.

Mean, immoral ones beg and don't repay;

Though the godly find enough to share.

Those the LORD will bless find true happiness

When they cultivate their land and play.

He protects, He directs

Faithful leaders and the steps they take.

He delights day and night

In the detail of the lives they make.

Once, how young I was! Though, I'm older now,

I have never seen the righteous fall.

Though they miss commands, He upholds their hands.

God presides, and He will make them stand.

Never renounced!

God's own children never beg for bread

Turned back, never!

Godly children are a joy instead.

Turn from evil temptations, miscreants,

Do your good to build a legacy!

For the LORD esteems just and righteous means

He will not forsake you, trust and see.

Leaning, leaning,

Safe and secure from all alarm

Leaning, leaning,

Leaning on the everlasting arms!

He will keep our souls safe forevermore,

Watch the godly spread throughout their lands!

I have seen the tree of the wicked man

Cut down, then he vanished, look again!

Leaning, leaning,

Safe and secure from all alarm

Leaning, leaning,

Leaning on the everlasting arms!

Share this counseling, teach them right from wrong;

'Til they make the law of God their own,

Then they'll never slip from His path for them.

He will lead them all the way back home.

He will save, He will save,

Be a shelter in the bitter storm.

Look to those honest souls,

You'll discover peace and rich reward.

PSALM 38

(Penitent's Psalm to Remember a Suffering Sinner)
Tune: SHELTERED IN THE ARMS OF GOD
(I feel the touch of heaven so kind and tender)
Dottie Rambo (1965)

LORD, do not punish me with indignation,

Or discipline me in Your righteous wrath.

For arrows from Your bow have aimed and found me,

And Your strong hand is pressing heavily.

Oh, now Your anger saps

The health I had

In body and soul,

There's no strength left in my bones because I've erred.

Because my sins have piled high upon me,

They are the burdens I can hardly bear.

From foolishness, my wounds are foul and festering;

I'm mourning bent and bowed in suffering.

The burning of my soul is crushing over

And I groan and faint from fierce torment.

LORD, my desires are clear

They're obvious,

You see all my sighs.

I can't hide my racing heart or waning strength.

And even light within my eyes has faded.

And my loved ones stand far off from me.

Those setting snares to take my life and harm me,

They threaten to destroy me all day long;

Their treachery is plotted in my silence.

I do not try to bring my own defense.

I put my hope in You, LORD,

All my hope;

I know that You'll come through,

Oh LORD God, You heard my falling cry for help!

And, when I said, "Don't let them laugh and scorn me."

All that pride proves they don't care at all.

My pain is constant, anxiously reminding:

I confess my guilt and my delays.

But enemies have energy and power,

And they hate that I have now obeyed.

Lord, don't abandon me,

Oh, don't be far,

Hurry to my help!

Lord, my Savior, You're the God who will abide.

I'm leaning on Your promises to carry

Anyway You chose to save my life.

154

PSALM 39

(The Fleeting Nature of Life. For the Choir Director)
Tune: I'M A CHILD OF THE KING
(MY FATHER IS RICH IN HOUSES AND LANDS)
John B. Summer (1877) Public Domain

I determined to guard my choices and ways

To hinder reproach by what I have to say.

I was speechless as though I had muzzled my mouth

As long as the vile were lurking about.

    I was quiet with them, quiet with them,

    Even from goodness, I was quiet with them.

In silence, my pain, like fire grew hot,

It only intensified my musing thoughts.

So, finally I spoke: "LORD, won't You display

The end of my life and my number of days?

    Oh LORD, let me know how quickly life goes!

    For we have a life span like a vapor below.

Purposeless souls seem to hurry in fear,

They hurry about chasing shadows and mirrors.

They gather up heaps of possessions for naught.

They die unaware of who gets what they bought.

    For what do I wait? LORD, why do I wait?

    My hope is in You, LORD! Not with these vain

    things.

Rescue me, LORD! I've trespassed again,

And now my transgressions let fools apprehend.

Then, You followed and grabbed me and disciplined hard

I've kept my mouth shut, I am speechless, oh, LORD!

    Smother Your heat; consuming conceits,

    And fading, I know we are vapors deceived.

"Will You listen, oh LORD, to my cries, to my prayer?

I'm desperate for help, don't ignore all my tears.

For I am a guest and a foreigner, too,

Like my fathers before were residing with You.

    Look away from your route with me in Your path.

    Oh, will You assure me, I won't die in Your wrath?"

PSALM 40

(Thanksgiving and a Cry for Help
For the choir director.)
Tune: FILL MY CUP, LORD
Richard Blanchard (1964)

So, I waited patiently for the LORD GOD.

He turned to me and heard my cry.

He brought me out of desolation,

Up from the muddy bog that cupped my life!

Then He set me

Upon a high rock,

Set my feet to make my footing sure.

Put a new song in my mouth, a hymn of praise

To our God, able LORD, the One we serve!

Oh, how happy is the one who has trusted

Completely, only in the LORD.

A soul who cannot be distracted

By a pride of life the others hold!

LORD my Sovereign,

Your deeds are awesome!

Many signs reveal Your plans are sweet!

Any other's deed from ruler, helper, love,

None compare, You redeem, and You complete.

Neither sacrifice nor offering delight You

As when I listen for Your voice.

"Now, I have come to pay attention;

For, I'm written in Your book of choice!

I delight to

Do Your will, LORD,

You're my God; Your purpose lives inside."

I declare how good and just You always are!

In the crowds, there, my witness will reside!

You've credited my ledger, I tell them.

I speak about Your gracious face:

My Savior and a Faithful Presence,

I don't hide Your every saving grace!

Love and truth, LORD,

They guard my life, LORD,

And Your great compassion is my verse!

In the great assembly I will speak my mind,

For, oh LORD, You are kind to be my worth.

Untold troubles in this time still surround me;

My sins have caught me up again;

I search, but cannot find an answer

To concerns, too numerous to land!

Lack of courage

Leaves me forfeit;

LORD, be pleased— again— to see me through!

Oh, be quick! and, hurry to my aid, dear LORD!

Come deliver. Oh, now to me be true.

Take Your mercies from the paths of controllers

Who rake my future through their hands;

Let them, in turn, be found disgraceful,

And confound their harmful scheming plans.

Let the mockers,

The finger pointers,

Be humiliated in Your zeal

Let their shameful ways return and bring chagrin,

Let their shame and their horror be revealed.

Oh, let all who seek Your face find rejoicing.

May these be glad in Your embrace;

Let all who love Your full salvation,

Find their constant voice in what we say,

"You are great, LORD!

He is the great LORD!"

I present my woeful needs today;

But the LORD is thinking of me. He's my help;

So, deliver, LORD! Do not delay!

PSALM 41

(A Psalm for the Compassionate and Kind)
Tune: IN THE SWEET BY AND BY
(There's a Land that is Fairer than Day)
Joseph P. Webster (1868)

There is joy for the kindhearted soul

Who brings help to the enduring poor;

For the LORD comes with power to save

When the kind also come to implore.

Troubles come to us all,

But the LORD is the sure guarantor;

He gives shelter and aid,

And He blesses with life evermore.

So He prospers the land of the kind,

And He rescues them from evil hands.

And the LORD nurses when they are sick

And restores them to health by command.

"Oh, have mercy!" I pray,

"Heal me where sin has entered and stayed.

I have strayed far from You."

But deceivers make up a crusade.

They are drumming their fingers for death.

"Tell us when he is gone and forget!"
Yet, they visit me like we were friends,
While they spread poison gossip and fret.
Trusted friend, man of peace,
Whom I trusted completely, has turned;
LORD, have mercy, I pray.
Make me well, vindicate me today!

Like a rain filling footprints of dread,
Double crossing and murmurs of death
They've discarded my frail silhouette.
"He will never get out of that bed!"
Trusted friend, peaceful friend,
Whom I trusted completely has turned;
LORD, have mercy, I pray.
Make me well, vindicate me today!

You assured me Your fealty of love,

And Your pleasure in me You've affirmed;

You've preserved me in my innocence

And their tracks of predictions You spurned!

Praise the LORD, Praise the LORD!

God of Israel, who lives without end!

He is life evermore;

No beginning, no ending, a-men!

~BOOK TWO~

(PSALMS 42–72)

PSALM 42

Tune: IN LOVING-KINDNESS JESUS CAME
(OH PRAISE HIS NAME, HE LIFTED ME)
Charles H. Gabriel Chicago, Illinois (1905)

A desperate deer for streams of drink,

Is how I long for You, my King!

I thirst for You, the living God.

When can I stand with Him?

My heart is crushed by sneering wolves.

All day and night I lick my tears

While faithless peers go on and on,

"Where is this God you say is yours?"

The vivid memories of a time

Remind me of a paradigm;

I walked among the worshipers,

And led a great parade!

The house of God would welcome us;

We sang for joy and gave Him thanks

Amid the sounds of joyful fun,

We celebrated, with our praise!

So, why my heart, be sad and down?

I feel discouragement rebounds!

Yet, I will put my hope in God!

I'll praise my Savior's name!

Again, from distant mountain peaks

my Savior-God pours His relief.

Now I'm discouraged, yet the source

Of Jordan's tides will surge for me.

And I remember crashing seas,

The tumult of a breaking frieze

Your raging love unfailing soared

In waves that swept for me!

Now every day my loyal LORD

Is pouring down unfailing love,

And so I sing His songs alone

Through every night in grateful tones.

"O God who gives me steadfast life, —
Why have You left me in this night?
Why must I wander in my grief,
Oppressed by enemies?"
Their taunting breaks my lowly bones.
They scoff, "Where is this God of yours?"
And, why am I cast down again?
I choose to hope in God alone!

PSALM 43

(Written by the sons of Korah, in sequel to Psalm 42)
Tune: I WOULD BE TRUE
Joseph Y. Peek (1911)
Alternate tune: "Intercessor" Charles H. H. Parry (1904)

Oh, God, declare a verdict in my favor!

Count me as innocent from unjust lies!

Defend my honor with Your vindication!

Rescue me from these grand imperious lies!

Rescue me from these grand imperious lies.

I come to You, for God, You are my Haven.

You are my Safety, there is none like You!

Why have You tossed me out to this oppression?

Why must I wander in this grieving place?

Why must I wander in this grieving place?

Send out Your light and truth, oh let them lead me;
Let them be guides to light my way above!
There, to Your holy mountain where You're living
There, to the altar of my gracious God!
There, to the altar of my gracious God.

O God, the source of all my joy and playing,
Praising You with my harp and all its strings.
Oh, God, my God! Why am I still discouraged?
Why is my heart still groping for my hope?
I'll praise my Savior-judge Who gives me hope!

PSALM 44

(A Corporate Lament, without confession written by the Sons of Korah)
Tune: FAIREST LORD JESUS (BEAUTIFUL SAVIOR)
"Crusader's Hymn" Silesian folk song from Schlesische
Volkslieder (1842), arranged by Richard S. Willis (1850)

Oh, YAHWEH, we have heard

Testimonies in our ears

Of our ancestors' faithful words;

Tales of the olden days

In which You made a way.

Your power cleaned up pagan lands!

After You drove them out,

Crushing nations with Your power,

You freed our ancestors, gave them ground,

They did not conquer it

With their own swords or wit;

But it was Your right hand and strength!

They give You all the praise

With their own strong arms upraised;

Victors, You showed them a full display!

Your blinding face in light

Helped them dispel the night,

How well You loved them then, always!

YAHWEH, my God and King,

Orchestrating triumph's ring,

Conquering all by authority.

Pushing back enemies

By Your supremacy;

In Your great name we trample foes!

I do not trust my bow;

Inventoried blades, oh no!

These weapons won't blaze our salvation.

You are the Saving One,

Unique to all nations,

You bring disgrace upon their war.

O God, we give You praise
Unrequited in Your name,
Your glorious praises, we sing all day!
But when our fortune changed,
We watched You toss away
Our honor for dishonor made!

Why do You no longer lead?
Now our troops flee in retreat;
Armies to battle come beaten home!
Rascals come plunder lands
Given us by Your hand,
You let them butcher us like lambs!

Scattered throughout the world,
Nations claimed us unobserved;
You sold, in short sales, Your precious ones!
And, in the aftershock
You let our neighbors mock
As objects of derision's scorn.

We were made the butt of jokes;

You imprisoned us like rogues.

Indignities we could not escape!

Is this Your covenant?

We did not bow to them.

We loved Your Lordship and Your law.

You have crushed us in the wild

Of the jackal's desert pride

Covered in darkness and death we died.

If we had overreached

Your holy name impeached,

You would have known our secret hearts.

We have never cast our lot

With the prayers to foreign gods,

But for Your sake we are killed each day;

Slaughtered, we are, like sheep.

Wake up, O LORD! Don't sleep!

Why do You gaze the other way?

Rise up in our defense!

We've collapsed by Your consent!

Oh, don't extinguish Your precious ones!

Still You neglect our wounds,

Suffered by brutes' abuse!

Oh, help us, ransom us in love!

PSALM 45

(Sons of Korah, For the Conqueror's Royal Wedding)
Tune: I'D RATHER HAVE JESUS THAN SILVER OR GOLD
Rhea F. Miller (1922) Public Domain

My ardor is stirring a verse so fine

Befitting the King in a noble incline,

And, I am immersed in a noble theme

Coming quick to my tongue with a skillful stream.

"With Your striking looks, the most handsome kind,

You have won all crowns combined!

Your lips are dripping with gracious words

For our God has blessed Your throne.

Take up Your broadsword, oh, Mighty One!

This warrior majestic, who shines as the sun!

And robed in Your majesty, out You ride

To a victory's claim, to defend the tried:

Truth and Meekness with all Just routines,

You defend with arrows keen.

May Your hand achieving inspiring deeds,

Putting nations at Your feet.

YAHWEH, forever Your throne endures:

Oh, King, You rule with a scepter of truth;

How You love integrity; hate disgrace.

And above all else, God has set Your place.

    He is pouring oil of myrrh and joy,

    On your robes as music plays!

    Perfuming with aloes and cassia too

    In Your ivory palaces.

The princesses live in Your palace rooms.

Upon Your right hand, the queen brightly blooms;

She's wearing the jewelry from Ophir's vaults.

It is golden and gleams with a fine emboss!

    Won't the royal daughter take to heart;

    Will she hear what I would say?

    Forget your people so far away

    Take your royal Husband's part.

Let the King delight in your fairest form;

Won't you give Him love, for He is your LORD?

And Tyre's cities will shower gifts

And the wealthy will beg of your favored lips.

    Oh, the royal bride, looks glorious! —

    In her flowing golden gown!

    In robes embroidered, she's led to Him,

    To her King, enthused and crowned.

From the joy-filled chambers the virgins leap

Sweeping in procession this bride to the King.

Your sons will be rulers with traits like Him.

You will make them to rule over many lands.

    I will lift Your noble name through time

    With praise in every line!

    Your honor forever will bear You up

    As the realms forever chime.

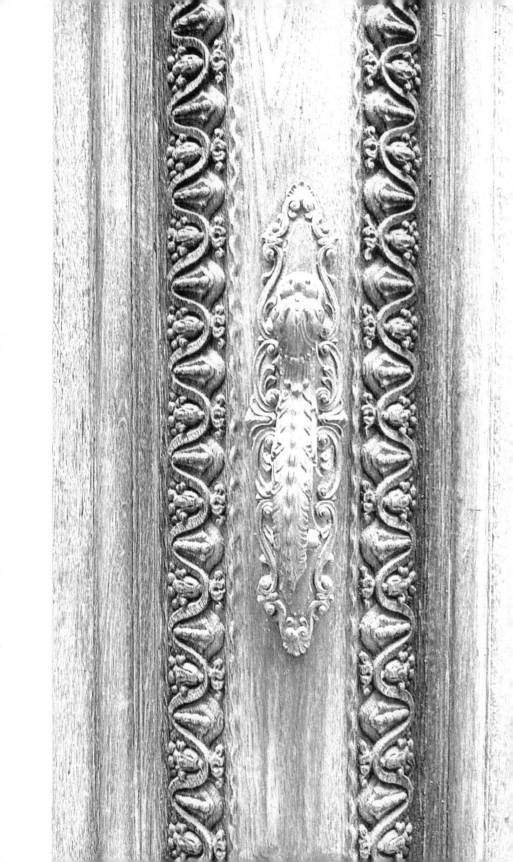

PSALM 46

(The Safety of God. A Psalm of Faith by the Sons of Korah)
Tune: ONWARD CHRISTIAN SOLDIERS
"St. Gertrude," Arthur S. Sullivan (1871)

God is Sanctuary! He's our refuge strong,

Ever-present Help for trouble all day long!

Knowing this, all fear is gone,

Though the earth gives way,

Though the summits crumble,

Though they slip into the bay.

Though the waters roar and foam and

Though the mountains quake,

There's a river flowing that will keep us safe!

There in holy dwellings thrives a city fair.

There the Most High lives with each within His care.

He will help her, He will save

At the break of day.

Nations roar and kingdoms melt, and

At His voice, they fray.

Angel armies stand His ground encircling His own.

Come and see what Jacob's LORD of Hosts has done!

Desolations He has brought and deserts to the earth.

He makes peace and ceasefires,

Shatters weapons' worth,

Burns the vicious tools of war,

Comforts with His rod:

"Just let go, be quiet now, and

Know that I am God.

I will be exalted in earth in every race."

Jacob's LORD Almighty is our safest place!

PSALM 47

(A Royal Psalm, A Victory Psalm of Praise by the Sons of Korah)
Tune: JESUS LOVES EVEN ME
(I AM SO GLAD THAT JESUS LOVES ME!)
Philip P. Bliss (1870)

Come, everyone! Come and clap your hands!

Shout out to God with a loud jubilance!

YAHWEH, the Most High, inspires this awe;

He is the King of all earth; sing *hurrah*!

As we approach, He crumbles our foes,

Beneath our feet, are nations deposed.

He chose the Land He promised to us:

Jacob's inheritance!

God has ascended with shouts full of joy;

YAHWEH ascended with trumpeted noise!

The proud possession of Jacob's descents,

Inherit land for He loves all of them.

Sing to our God, sing praises to Him;

Sing to our King, in rhythms and hymns!

God is the King, He rules over earth.

Praise Him with wisdom's psalms.

God reigns above every culture and state;

Sitting on His holy throne, He dictates.

Rulers of all the world's best have convened

Gathered with Abraham's children esteemed.

Nobles and stars belong to the LORD,

Leaders of earth to this Unique God.

He is the One most highly esteemed

Honor Him everywhere!

PSALM 48

(A Hymn of Praise by the Sons of Korah)
Tune: GRACE THAT IS GREATER THAN ALL OUR SIN!
Daniel B. Towner (1910)

YAHWEH is great and is greatly praised

From His great city known to deploy.

His holy mountain, of splendid heights,

Graces the whole earth with sweeping joy!

Zion's Mountain,

Up on the slopes of the northern peak,

Lies the great King's

City of citadels fortified.

See how the kings of the world have come

Gathered for war, advancing as one.

Look! When they saw it, they marveled here;

Fleeing in agony, seized with fear.

Writing terrors,

Pains of a woman in labor's grip,

Mauled by east winds,

Tarshish is doomed as He wrecks her ships.

Just as we heard it, so we have seen

Inside the mountain of the great King

Flourishing city with God's rapport;

God will establish it evermore!

Oh, God, inside

Your holy temple, we contemplate

Your love, faithful,

Reaches the ends of the earth in praise.

May You be praised as the Faithful God;

"Faithful our God, forever to lead!"

Your ruling right hand is Just for all.

Mount Zion smiles and Judah calls.

Go around Zion,

Circle it, counting its tower walls;

Note its ramparts;

May ages know God is overall!

PSALM 49

(The Foolishness of Trusting in Riches)
Tune: IT CAME UPON A MIDNIGHT CLEAR
"Carol," Richard S. Willis (1850)
Alternate tune: "Noel," Arthur S. Sullivan (1871)

Hear this, all nations of the world;

You great and small in heart,

You rich and poor together hear

My wisdom on the harp!

My meditation shall be clear

As understanding prose:

The proverb and the riddle sing

As I explain them both:

Why should I fear when danger comes

Confounded enemies, —

The ones who put their trust in wealth

And boast iniquities?

For no one's assets can redeem

The price of human life;

Each costly soul is ransomed by

Our God who sets its price.

What could we pay that God would trade

To let us out-live time?

Immortal like, enjoying life

In rich estates sublime?

For one can see that wise ones die,

And fools, they all pass away.

They leave their wealth to other hands.

Their homes becomes their graves.

Estates are named to flatter pride

Of pompous heirs below

But generations pass on by

Those silent wealthy bones.

Despite one's wealth, the flesh won't last;

For humans die like herds;

There goes the path of the arrogant,

And those who follow their words.

As sheep are destined for the pit,

Decay will shepherd the proud.

Yet, morning casts its waking light

Where those of virtue are crowned.

Conceited forms will waste away

Far from their lofty estates.

But God will fully redeem my life

From powers of the grave.

The LORD will take me, I'm not afraid;

And neither should you fear!

For some get rich, and homes increase,

But when they die, it's clear:

A soul takes nothing to the grave,

Releasing wealth and pride.

Though self-made men are lavished praise,

Their souls will never see light.

PSALM 50

(A Psalm of Asaph. God is the Mighty Savior, Judge, not a human)
Tune: ARE YOU WASHED IN THE BLOOD?
Elisha A. Hoffman (1878)
Public Domain

Hear the Mighty Savior, He's our God and LORD;

He has spoken and called to the earth!

From the sun's arising to its going down,

Out of Zion, our God's shining forth!

Oh, His face! Satisfies!

God is now being seen on return;

There's a fire spreading out before His robes,

From His feet, like a tempest, it burns.

He shall call the heavens from His throne above;

Call to earth, that in time, He may judge.

Call His own together: "Gather all My saints

Be with me, now in good governance!

Oh, this Love! Satisfies!

Covenants cover each I have touched!

You who rested on them by My sacrifice."

Let the heavens declare God is Judge!

"Hear, My people, listen, I will tell you all,

Hear Me, Israel, I speak to your guilt;

I *am* God, your Father, so I will not fault

You for spilling the blood you have spilled.

Sacrifices are burnt,

Constant offerings you make for my sake.

But, I don't ask from you and I do not take

Sacrifices from your meager gates.

Now remember, every forest beast, though wild,

To the last of the cattle is Mine!

I know every mountain bird and every song,

In My thousands of hills all aligned.

"If I'd thirst, if I'd starve, —

Why would I call on you or complain?

For the earthly fullness *is* My own to take,

It belongs to My splendid domain!

Will I eat an offering you've burned in sin?

Would I drink of the blood of your goat?

What I want is thankfulness, your sacred best;

Not a scapegoat to bless the Most High.

Pay your vows to Me now;

Call on Me in your day of distress;

I'll deliver timely and I'll help you out!

Then you'll splendidly be My success!"

Oh, to evil plotters of your wayward ways

"Where's your *right*," He demands, "to declare—

To determine My statutes, or My covenants?

Without me, you interpret from air!

And you cast all My words

On the ground, spitting out from behind.

When a thief came by you, you consented too,

And adultery has kept you confined.

By deceitful judgments you give in to wrong,

And you slander your sibling removed!

In your mother's sorrow, I kept silent too.

But you mistook My silence for proof;

I rebuke you, and now

I will reset the prior design!

What was My designation, I will bring to pass

I will right the wrongs, and re-score.

"Now consider this, in running without God,

Lest I tear *you* to pieces and bones.

There'll be none delivering and none to save!

You forget Who deserves to be known.

Will you now offer praise?

Bring me glory and bring joyful awe!

And whoever orders life in conduct *aright*

I will show the salvation of God."

PSALM 51

(David's Penitent Psalm after his adultery with Bathsheba and
orchestrating the murder of her husband)
Tune: ABIDE WITH ME FAST FALLS THE EVENTIDE
Henry Lyte (1847)

Have mercy, God! Have mercy on this soul!

My hopeless being leans on Your sweet control.

Your many mercies cover all my deeds.

Wash me completely and I will be clean!

My rebel acts confront me day and night

What I have done is evil in Your sight.

Against You only does my sinning wrong.

Your words have proved correct, Your justice strong.

Though You are blameless, I was born in sin.

Though You are just, Your constancy will win.

Your tender mercies called me in the womb.

There, taught me honesty and wisdom too.

Blot out my guilt and clean my inward part.

Scrub out the stain of hardness in my heart.

I will be whiter, brighter than the snow!

Fill me with gladness, 'til Your joy I know.

YAHWEH, create in me a pure envoy,

My broken spirit lacks my Savior's joy.

Do not abandon, do not bar me, LORD!

Bring back vitality and open doors.

When You restore the joy of saving grace,

LORD, make me willing, guide me to my place.

Following Your directives from the start,

Rebels who turn to listen gain Your heart.

Forgive me, God of Judgment, for my wrongs:

Shedding of blood by schemes and cunning arms!

Oh, God who saves me; joyfully I sing

Of Your forgiveness in the praise I bring.

You don't desire fire sacrifice,

   No burning smoke no incense when I cry.

My contrite heart is what Your heart desires.

   You seek repentance, in the eyes of Zion.

Look on with favor, make Your kingdom come!

   Build up the walls of old Jerusalem.

Then we will please You, sacrificing bulls

   Offered in righteousness upon altars.

PSALM 52

(God is True to His Name. For The Choir Director: A Davidic Maskil.
When Doeg the Edomite went and reported to Saul,
telling him, "David went to Ahimelech's house.")
Tune: IN THE SWEET BY AND BY (There's a Land
that is Fairer than Day)
Joseph P. Webster (1860)

So you brag of what evil can bring

In your mighty and steamy extremes?

Though your traction appears to be keen,

God will take center stage and be seen.

For His goodness is sure

It will outlive the cruel, and endure!

Faithfulness out performs;

God is Sovereign, oh, He will be sure!

As a razor is sharpened to raze

So your tongue loves to find evil ways

To destroy with your words and betray,

Forging lies, for the love of the play.

God remains provident!

He uproots you clean out of your tent!

Then, the righteous will see

And will mock you in breathless assent.

This fine person would not hide in God

For he trusted his riches instead.

In the wake of abundance and sin,

He made evil a fortress of whims.

This is me: olive tree,

Flourishing in the house of my God!

I will wait, I will trust

In my awe of the kindness of Love!

I will trust in Your good covenant;

In the presence of Your faithful ones,

I will praise You for what You have done,

For Your name brings me hope I can trust:

In the High covenant

You are awesome and fierce for Your love,

You are true to defend

Those who love You and love Your commands.

PSALM 53

Tune: I HEARD THE BELLS ON CHRISTMAS DAY
John Baptiste Calkin (1848)
To be sung antiphonally by a leader and a chorus:

The fool repeats down in his heart,

"There is no God to disregard."

These fools are vile, their ways corrupt;

And, no one gives an afterthought.

Our God is looking down from heaven

To see if any understand,

Of human kind, do any plan

To seek their true Designer's hand?

See, everyone has turned away,

Corrupted, they have disobeyed;

No one does good, not even one.

Do crooked see they are undone?

Will evil people never dread?

    They eat my people's life like bread!

They never think to call on God.

    When terror comes, then comes a rod.

The wicked, overwhelmed with dread,

    Turned back when God drew near, and fled.

He scattered those betrayers' bones

    Who violated you alone.

Oh, make salvation come of Zion,

    and Israel benefit on high!

When God restores our joy to laugh,

    Let Jacob shout on his behalf!

PSALM 54

(For the Director of Music. With stringed Instruments.
A Maskil and Lament of David.
When the Ziphites had gone to Saul and said,
"Is not David hiding among us?")
Tune: FAITH OF OUR FATHERS, LIVING STILL
"St. Catherine,"
arranged by James G. Walton (London:1864)

Save me, O God, by Your living name.

Command all strength to vindicate blame!

Hear this my prayer, oh, my God, hear my plea;

Listen to all the words I complete.

Arrogant foes have tracked me down;

Ruthless, without regard for God.

Certainly, God must be near to my pain;

He is the LORD, the One who sustains!

Let wicked slanderers' traps become sprung;

Cause them to cease, destroy everyone.

LORD, to Your faithfulness be true!

Render their ruins Your revenue.

Now in my freedom I'll sacrifice
Over, above, expected tithes;
Now, I am praising Your matchless name
For You made good for Your acclaim.
When I looked up, I saw my foes
Thrashing in pangs of troubled woe.

Psalm 55

(For the director of music. With stringed instruments.
A *Maskil* and Lament of David.)
Tune: SILENT NIGHT
Franz Xaver Gruber (1818)

Hear, oh God, Hear my cry!

Do not turn from my sigh;

Hear and answer my troubled thoughts.

Hear and answer me, I am distraught.

By my enemy's sayings,

And by his meaningful threats.

Vicious degrees of suffering,

He assails, in sweeping wails!

Now, I languish in terrible death

Anguish follows me, fear has beset.

Horror! Trembling has claimed me.

Oh, for the wings of a dove!

Fly away, far away,

    I would fly, find a place.

In the desert, I'd stay in a nest,

    Sheltered safe from the tempest in chase

Hurry up to my shelter,

    From a tumultuous storm.

Oh, LORD, confuse their wicked ruse,

    For I see violent streets.

There is strife in the city I love.

    Day and night they are prowling its walls;

    Malice and menacing handshakes

    Willing to kill and destroy.

If it were strange enemy's rage

    I'd endure, I'd endure;

Given a foe was arising, I'd hide.

    Could this be a companion I liked?

    You, were my partner and close friend!

    Someone I always enjoyed.

Walking about, all through God's house
  Fellowshipping confidents
All the worshipers, who were our friends,
    Allies always, without a pretense.
  Oh, may death appear frightening!
    Let them go visit the dead!

As for my part, I'm calling to God;
  Watch the LORD save me now!
I am bellowing morning and night;
    In distress, though He's hearing my voice,
  Quickly coming to rescue,
    Saving me from battle cries.

Many oppose him, though He knows,
  Yet my God, stays the same!
Never ending, enthroned of old,
    He will hear and will humble the bold,
  Those who live without fearing,
    Fear this, my God on His throne!

My old friend tackled his friends;

    Breeching over covenants.

While his lips were as smooth as silk,

      War moved out in his heart of guilt,

    Words more soothing than oil,

      Yet they were drawn with a sword.

Oh, cast your cares onto the LORD,

    He will never let you down!

He will keep and sustain His own;

      Cast your troubles on Him and be found.

    YAHWEH cares for the righteous,

      You, too, may trust in my God.

God will cull hostile souls,

    Send to pits of decay.

All the blood thirsty souls in deceit

      Will not thrive many days on their feet.

    As for me, I will trust You.

      Yes, I will trust in my God.

PSALM 56

(For the choir director: David's lyric when the Philistines seized him in Gath) A Miktam "inscription" or "to cover."
Tune: ARE YE ABLE? SAID THE MASTER
Harry S. Mason (1924)

Oh, YAHWEH, show me mercy!

From the stalkers storming me,

Hostile people keep pursuing,

You see them constantly!

I'm hounded by slander, it's cunning and strong!

When I am afraid, I'll hold You in my song,

Trusting and praising the promise of God,

For why should I fear what mortals can do wrong?

There are always some distorters,

Twisting what I say and do;

    They will spend their days of spying

Finding how to pierce me through.

Bind the absconders from finding Your home!

God, just in anger, bring them quickly down!

You're keeping track of my sorrows and plight.

For You have collected all these tears in life.

Every tear, LORD, You have saved them

in your bottle— saved my cries.

    You've recorded every teardrop

In the book that You transcribe.

As I was calling for Your aid and peace,

I found them fallen! All my enemies!

This much I know now, God is on my side!

I praise Him completely; for He has never lied!

And beyond this, how I praise Him,
For He's promised mighty aid.
    Since I trust in God, Almighty,
Why should I be afraid?
How can mere mortals bring trouble on me? —
Fulfilling my vows, for You are greatly pleased.
To You, oh, Father, I'm offering thanks
In my sacrifices for Your saving grace!

You have kept me from an ending;
You have kept my tearful notes
    You have kept my feet from slipping,
And my trust did not misquote.
Now in Your presence, oh, God, we converse!
I'm walking beside You, bringing praising verse.
Now in Your presence, in life-giving light.
Completely, I know as fully I have sight.

PSALM 57

(A Lament of David, to the Hebrew tune: "Do Not Destroy."
A *miktam.* "inscription" or "to cover."
When he fled from Saul into the cave. For the director of music.)
Tune: I Need Thee Every Hour (I Need Thee, Oh I Need Thee!)
Robert Lowry (Cincinnati, Ohio,1872)

Have mercy, gracious God, show mercy over me,

For only You provide a shelter this complete.

I'm hiding in the shadows,

Shadows of Your pinions

Until the full disaster has passed from view.

I'm crying out to God, Almighty, Most High,

To God, who vindicates me, I will bring my plight.

He sends to save from heaven, halting those who chase me

He commandeers His love and His faithfulness!

I'm living in the midst of ravenous beasts;

I'm forced among the men with arrows for teeth

Oh, God, exalt Your glory, now above the heavens.

Above their sharpened tongues, let Your glory abide!

They spread a net to catch my careful, fleeing feet;

I'm bowing in distress and downed because of heat.

My path, they marked and shoveled

Pits to catch me headlong;

But they have fallen into their pits themselves!

My steadfast heart! My heart is steadfast,

And O, my God, it's steady with a song.

In early hours singing, pleasing You with music!

Awake, my soul at dawn with the zither and harp!

I'll praise You, Adonai, among the other tribes;

Beginning with a song, Your praise is glorious.

Amazing is Your great love, over every heaven!

Your faithfulness abounding on earth into skies.

PSALM 58

(For the director of music. To the Hebrew tune: "Do Not Destroy." David's
Miktam "inscription" or "to cover.")
Tune: HAVE YOU ANY ROOM FOR JESUS?
He Who Bore Your Load of Sin
C. C. Williams (1878)
Alternate Tune: ALL THE WAY, MY SAVIOR LEADS ME

Are you righteous in your rulings?

Are you fairly judging all?

Speak proficiently in detail?

No, confusion is your call!

You seek only your advantage,

And injustice with your hands;

Meted out for spreading violence

On the earth in wicked plans.

Early from a crooked birth place,

From the womb they go astray.

They will go their way perversely,

Spreading lies and giving chase.

Wicked venom is the venom

Of a serpent without ears.

It ignores the charmer's tunes and

Odd enough, it cannot hear.

Take the bite from lions' roaring!

Break the teeth inside their mouths.

Let them flee like frothing spillage

Take their purpose, close their jowls.

When they aim their maiming arrows

Sweep them from the targets sought.

May they be a prowling slug that

Melts before it moves along.

Soon, before Your kettle boils

Fueled by tinder sticks and thorns,

Wicked ones will slip away and

Sweep with them the old and young.

God will soon avenge the righteous!

They will celebrate their cause,

When they dip their feet in blood from

Pooling souls whom God has judged.

PSALM 59

(For the director of music. To the Hebrew tune: "Do Not Destroy." David's
Miktam. "inscription" or "to cover."
When Saul had sent men to watch David's house in order to kill him.)
Tune: I MUST TELL JESUS ALL OF MY TRIALS
Elisha A. Hoffman (1893)

Save me, oh save me, God, from the wicked;

Be my True Fortress from their elite.

Save me, oh God, from those who do evil;

Rescue me from those thirsty for blood.

See, they conspire, see how they lie there!

Waiting for me, these fierce-some of foes!

For no offense, LORD, I am a pure one,

Yet they lie down, awaiting and strong.

Arise to help me; look on my plight, LORD,

You are Almighty, You who are God.

Rousing Yourself to punish the nations;

Show them no mercy, traitors and hounds.

Prowling about the city, they snarl;

When they return at evening like dogs,

See how they spew from mouths that are caverns

Words from their lips are sharper than swords!

Although they think, "Whoever can hear us?"

You LORD, are laughing, scoffing their moves;

Scoffing at all those nations opposing,

You are my Strength, I watch Your reproof!

Almighty fortress, You are my Fortress,

You are my God on Whom I rely.

Moving before me, routing their slander,

You are my God on Whom I rely.

Oh, Sovereign LORD, these people are Yours and

Though You uproot them, bringing them down,

They are my people, so do not kill them,

They would forget that You are our Shield.

Yet, for the sins they sin with their mouths, and

Words of their lips, so caught in their pride.

For all their lying, curses, and slander,

LORD, in Your wrath, consume all their pride.

Then it will spread and be known in Jacob,

Over the ends of the earth it will spread,

News that the God of Israel is Sovereign,

And they will wander, howling for food.

Prowling about the city, they snarl;

When they return at evening like dogs,

Yet, I will sing Your strength in the morning,

Yes, I will sing Your Fortress of Love.

PSALM 60

(A Corporate Lament, without confession)
A Miktam "inscription" or "to cover."
Tune: ALL TO JESUS I SURRENDER (I SURRENDER ALL)
W.S. Weeden (1896)

YAHWEH, You have burst upon us

You've rejected us, oh, God;

    With Your earthquakes in Your wrath You

Shook our lands and tore us up;

Now, restore our earth! Mend our fractured ground!

It is quaking, we are quaking, You have brought us down.

You, oh, God, have shown Your people,

Shown Your people desperate times;

    You have given us a wine that

Makes us stagger, makes us cry.

Yet the Auctioneer, cares for those who fear.

You have raised a banner for us, raised our hopes on high.

Raised, unfurling in the battle,

Now against their bows we rise.

    Save us, with Your right hand help us,

Let the ones who love You thrive.

God has spoken from heights of radiance,

Hear the Victor's voice in razing Mesopotamians.

"I will measure off the Valley

Of the central Syrians.

    Gilead and My Manasseh,

They are mine and they will live;

Helmet for the war: this is Ephraim.

Judah is My sovereign scepter, ruling monolith."

"Moab is My washing basin,

Edom is My careless floor.

    I will toss My sandal there and

Philistia, I abhor.

Shout in triumph shout! Over them I shout.

This is My decree to bring you safety in the war."

Who will bring me to the city fortified in Edom's land?

Is it not You, God, who left us

    Who rejected us firsthand?

You no longer aid armies we send forth!

Give us aid against the foe, for human help is sand.

Tag: God will gain the victory for us; He will trample down our foes.

PSALM 61

(A Royal Psalm of David, for the director of music. With stringed
instruments.)
Tune: NO ROOM, ONLY A MANGER OF HAY
John W. Peterson (1958)

Listen,

Listen, O God, hear my cry.

Listen to my petition and sigh.

From the ends of the earth I have called,

My courage failing;

Lead me;

Onto the rock I will climb.

One God, You are my refuge on high;

For You granted me refuge before,

A stronger tower!

    I long

    To dwell here forever,

    Under Your cover and shelter,

    And to be safe in the refuge of Your

    wing!

For You've

Listened, oh God, and You've heard

My vows, true to the witness observed;

And strong testaments in legacy;

Your name, they clung to.

Will You

Prolong the King's living days,

Give Him more generations of praise?

May He rule on His throne evermore

In God's good presence!

Appoint

Your fullest protection!

Truth and Your faithful affection.

Then I will sing evermore to praise

Your name!

Watch me

Filling my vows day by day;

Hear me singing the praise of Your name;

Watch me living a strong legacy.

My Rock is higher!

PSALM 62

(To the leader: according to Jeduthun. A Psalm of David.)
Tune: ALL THE WAY MY SAVIOR LEADS ME OR
(JESUS DOETH ALL THINGS WELL)
Robert Lowry (1890)
Alternate Tune: HAVE YOU ANY ROOM FOR JESUS?

Silently, my soul is waiting

For my God, and Him alone.

He's the One who brings salvation,

He's the founding Cornerstone.

He's my Fortress and Deliverer

I shall never lose my grip

He's my Judge, the LORD Almighty

My Defender and Defense.

On this God, I rest my honor,

He's my Strength and Recompense.

So, I taunt the mob assailing,

"How long will you push this wall?

Will you batter me your victim,

Like a barn of leaning stalls?"

For I know their simple aim is

Bringing nobles down with lies;

Their engaging stories slander

Taunting leaders prized and wise.

On the sly, they curse and slander

And in public sweetly smile.

Trust in Him, Oh people, always!

Pour your secrets out to God;

He's a refuge for the mighty,

He's a refuge for the flawed.

Those of low estate are vapors,

Those of high estate are air;

When it's over they expire

Weighed together in their err;

In the balance, they go rising;

Weighed together less than air.

Do not trust in good intentions,

In disguise a gift will tilt,

These assurances are empty,

Set no hope on robber's guilt;

If your riches seem increasing,

Do not set your heart on them.

For your future is in God's hands.

He has spoken, and it stands,

Paying fairly for your efforts,

He fulfills all His commands.

Silently, my soul is waiting

For my God, and Him alone.

He's the One who brings salvation,

He's the founding Cornerstone.

He's my Fortress and Deliverer

I shall never lose my grip

He's my judge, the LORD almighty

My defender, my Defense.

On this God, I rest my honor,

He's my strength and recompense.

PSALM 63

(A Lament of David, when he was in the Wilderness of Judah.) Tune:
AND CAN IT BE THAT I SHOULD GAIN?
"Sagina," Thomas Campbell (1825)

Oh God, my God, I'm desperate in the wild!

I languish for a taste of Your presence here;

See how my soul and my body faint,

In dry desert lands, weary, without drink?

So then, I gazed on You in the sanctuary,

Beholding

Your power

And lost in Your fame.

Your steadfast love surpasses life,

I bless Your name all my days and nights!

Lifting my hands, upon Your name I seize.

You satisfy my soul with the richest feast,

So in Your joy, I return Your praise

For You, only You, satisfy my days!

When on my bed, I am musing on Your Presence;

I meditate

On how You've helped

In watches of the night;

And in the shadow of Your wings

I sing for joy and to You I cling!

Your steady hand upholds me in the fight,

Diverting those who want to subdue my life.

They shall go down in the depths of earth;

Be given to perilous swords of death,

They are the prey for the jackals of the desert.

The holy King

Shall raise His voice

Rejoicing in His God!

All those who swear by Him shall leap,

Exulting liars cease to be!

PSALM 64

(For the director of music. A psalm of David.)
Tune: BE STILL MY SOUL
"Finlandia," Jean Sibelius, (1899)
Alternative tune: So Send I You
"Unde et Memores," William H. Monk, (1875)

Hear me, oh, God, I voice a raw complaint.

Will you protect me from the aberrant?

Oh, hide my life from those conspired behaviors!

Hide me from wicked plots of human will!

See how they sharpen tongues like arrows aiming

With cruel words of poison meant to kill?

They shoot in ambush at the purest victim;

Without considering, they shoot to kill!

Encouraged by the leaders planning evil;

They, in their plans, compare deceptive skills;

Then shrug and say, "Oh, who will ever see it?"

They plot injustice with a stunning will.

I am amazed, the human heart is cunning!

But God will shoot them with His arrows sure;

And suddenly, they will be stricken by Him.

Turning their tongues against themselves as spears!

He brings to ruin those who scheme destruction;

All see them now and mock their sore affairs.

All human life eventually will fear Him;

All will proclaim God's works and ponder well:

The righteous crowd will praise, rejoicing in Him,

For in the LORD, our refuge is fulfilled;

And all the upright hearts will glory in Him;

For He, in goodness, will reign as He should!

Psalm 65

(For the director of music. A psalm of David for Thanks and Exaltation)
Tune: HARK! THE HERALD ANGELS SING!
Felix Mendelssohn and William H. Cummings (1840)

Praise awaits You, God, in Zion;

Yes, to You all people come.

You, our God, will answer prayer,

For our vows in You, repair:

When in overwhelming sins,

You forgave our great transgressions.

Blessings rest on all You choose

Drawing near to live with You!

In Your courts and powerhouse

All good things do You endow.

God, You answer when we call

    God our Savior, hope of all!

Awesome deeds in righteous answers!

    to all peoples of the earth.

And to farthest seas You bring,

    Your good hope with awesome deeds!

You, who by Your power formed

    Mountain peaks with strengthened arms.

You, who stilled the roaring seas,

    made the nation's turmoil cease.

This whole earth is filled with awe

    At Your wonders; at Your songs!

Where does morning light deploy;

    Where does evening fade to joy?

You supply the land with water;

    You enrich it for our quota.

Yes, the streams of God are filled

    irrigating grain in fields

For all people You provide

    And ordain a yield for life.

Drenching furrows, and You level

    Ridges where You soften them

With the showers of Your blessing

  Of the crops that grow within.

So You crown the year with bounty,

  And Your carts, they're overflowing.

There the wild grasslands bloom;

  And the hills in glad costume,

While the meadows shout their voice

  Covered with their flocks in joy.

PSALM 66

For the director of music. Sing with three groups or soloists
Tune: ALAS! AND DID MY SAVIOR BLEED?
(AT THE CROSS, AT THE CROSS)
Ralph E. Hudson (1885)

With joy, all earth, come shout to God;

Sing glories of His name!

Oh magnify His praises rare;

To this, our God, proclaim:

    "Your acts and deeds! Your awesome feats;

    No, nothing can balance Your power!"

    Your enemies cringe for all in earth

    Consenting, will bow to sing Your worth!

Now, come and see what God has done,

His fruits to all bloodroot!

He turned the sea into dry land,

And they passed through on foot.

    Come, let's rejoice for fearsome grace;

    God rules supreme with power!

    And, always by His watching gaze

    The nations are endowed.

Come praise our God, each mother tongue,
Oh let His praise be heard!
He has preserved our very lives
And kept our feet assured.

      You tested us, oh God, in fire
      Refined to silver bowls;
      You brought us to our prison cells
      And bent our backs with loads.

Your servants bore down our backs;
We went through fire and flood,
Yet then You brought us to a place
Of opulent reward.

      I'm coming now to worship You
      To burn my firstborn bull,
      Your temple yet awaits my vow
      And promises in full.

When times were hard, I promised vows

In sacred sacrifice;

This fat from You, I offer back,

A ram to satisfy.

> The first of all belongs to You
>
> And this is for my good
>
> To bring into Your courts with praise
>
> the firstfruit of my herd.

Oh, come and hear, all you who fear

This God, and what he's done

For when I cried, He soon appeared

While praise was on my tongue.

> "Your acts and deeds! Your awesome feats;
>
> And all the earth will sing,
>
> For Who creates new life or wealth
>
> In harvest time or Spring?

If I'd preferred a heart of sin,

The LORD would not have heard

But God has surely listened well

And multiplied His word.

    All praises be to God, my God,

    Who did not lose my prayer!

    He showered love, did not withhold,

    The worth and all that's fair!

PSALM 67

(For the director of music. With stringed instruments. A praise song.)
Tune: GREAT IS THY FAITHFULNESS
William Marion Runyan (Baldwin Kansas, 1923)

May God be gracious to bless us and shine on;

Facing us, seeing us through mercy's eye

So that His ways may be known over all earth,

Whereby salvation comes to all mankind!

May people praise You!

All people praise You!

God, may the nations be glad in Your joy!

Gratefully singing for equity's wisdom,

Ruling and guiding the nations' deploy.

Earth yields a harvest as God, our God, blesses.

May He continue this happy chanson!

May all the nations oblige Him in fullness.

May they perceive their salvation is won!

> May people praise You!
>
> All people praise You!
>
> God, may the nations be glad and rejoice!
>
> Gratefully singing for equity's wisdom,
>
> Ruling and guiding the nations' deploy.

PSALM 68

(For the director of music. Of David. A psalm. A song.)
Tune: BE THOU MY VISION
"Slane," of Irish folk origin perhaps by St. Patrick 433
Alternate tunes: WHEN I SURVEY THE WONDROUS CROSS
Isaac Watts (1750) or Edward Miller (1790)
To be sung antiphonally by a leader and two choruses:

May God arise, may His enemies flee;

May they be scattered like smoky debris!

Blasting Your breath on them fairly it looms;

Melting as wax in the flame to consume!

May God arise, may the righteous delight!

May they, united, rejoice in God's sight;

May they be happy, enjoying His fame,

Singing to YAHWEH the praise of His name.

Let us extol Him who rides on the clouds!

Let us rejoice in His presence, aloud.

His name means Father, and Father of all,

Children without, on this Father may call.

God in His dwelling is holy, unique

    He defends widows, defenseless and weak,

And for the lonely, He plants them in love:

    Grants to a victim a family to trust.

God leads the prisoners to freedom with song!

    Let the rebellious burn where they belong

Inland with sun-scorching heat they will fade.

    He'll march His own through the desert to shade.

When You went out, God, to lead out Your own,

    How the earth tingled, how rain showered down!

Trembling for One Triune God in the storm,

    God of the Sinai, and Israel her horn!

Oh, God, You showered the rains to refresh

    Your weary people, and inheritance.

Your people settled in lands You bestowed

    Then from Your bounty, You settled the poor.

This LORD announces the Word in His land,
  Maidens throng 'round to proclaim it again.
"Kings leading armies flee turning in haste;
  Women at home split the plunder God gave."

"Even while sleeping out under the stars,
  My dove has wings sheathed with silvery bars;
Peacefully resting in rare feathers gold."
  LORD of the angels scattered kingdoms of old.

It was like Mount Zalmon's deep fallen snow,
  Mount Bashan's rugged majestic tableau.
Why fume in envy, you high mountain chains?
  This is God's summit where He deigns to reign.

These are the heights where the LORD makes His home.
  Chariots of God, with His angelic throne,
When the LORD comes from the Sinai to these,
  This sanctuary, He'll settle in peace.

When You ascended on high from the grave,

  Releasing captives, the many, to save;

Citizens offered allegiance in their gifts

  Even the hostile awarded respect.

Praise be to Adonai, Savior and God,

  Who bears our burdens, we praise and applaud.

This Sovereign loads us with benefits and boons

  And by Him comes all escapes from the tombs.

Surely, God crushes the heads of His foes,

  Crushing the crowns of the young high and low.

The LORD transmits them from Bashan to flood lands;

  Up from the deep seas, He wades in their blood.

God, Your procession has come into view,

  Heralds of singers are leading the queue;

Musicians, followed by young maidens drumming,

  Leading my King to His congregation!

In sanctuary, the great royal throngs
  Praise God in Israel and all Zebulun.
Princes of Naphtali, and Judah's might are
  Led by the true little Benjamin tribe.

Summon Your power, God, strength upon strength,
  Act as You famously have done at length!
Reign in Your temple in Jerusalem strong;
  Kings will bring tribute to You all day long.

Rebuke the beast in the reeds, and the bulls
  Standing in herds with the nations' young calves.
When You have humbled the beast, may it bring You
  Silver in bars as it bows to the King.

Scatter the nations who love to make war.
  Envoys from Egypt will come to implore;
Cush will submit herself also to our God.
  All earthly kingdoms will sing and applaud.

All praise to Him Who rides through heaven's skies,

Through highest heavens and throughout time, flies.

Sighing in thunder, proclaiming God's power,

Majesty reigns over Israel this hour!

You, God, are awesome, how awesome You are

Here in this place and residing in power!

This sanctuary is where God gives us strength.

High God of Israel summons power lead.

PSALM 69

(A Lament for the Falsely Accused and Isolated in Misery.
For the director of music. To the tune of "Lilies." Of David)
It is suggested to alternate the tunes below, and change up the choral
voicing for interest:
Tune: WHEN I SURVEY THE WONDROUS CROSS
Isaac Watts (1750) or Edward Miller (1790)
"Hamburg," Lowell Mason, (1824)
Alternate Tunes: BE THOU MY VISION "Eucharist," Isaac B. Woodbury
(1838)

Save me, oh, God, for the black waters rise,

Lapping my neck as I sink in the mire;

Into the depths, where no foothold I find,

Thrashing to find You in waters that rise.

As they engulf me, my throat becomes raw,

Parched, and I'm weary, LORD, please hear my call!

My eyes are failing to see God is good

Now, will He save me from new charges brewed?

My foes outnumber the hairs of my head!

So many hate me, yet they are misled!

What I did not take, now I must restore!

Seeking to ruin me, they're upping the score!

God, You know all of my folly and guilt.

You see my heart though it's covered with silt.

LORD the Almighty, may all those who hope

Find Your sweet favor, and not be reproached.

God, do not punish the pure for my sin;

Save those of Israel, and do not condemn!

Do not disgrace one who's seeking Your face;

Though I am shunned now and scorned for Your sake.

Treated as foreign among my own kin,

Even my siblings look on with chagrin;

This, for the zeal for Your house I'm consumed,

I bear the insults they mean against You.

While in my weeping and fasting I'm scorned;

While in my mourning, they make me their sport.

Those sitting up at Your welcoming gate

Mock me, poetically, while drunkards debate.

Still, I continue to pray to You, LORD,
For in the time of Your favor and love,
Your love was great, oh, my God, You were good;
So, answer me now in Your true livelihood.

Rescue me, now, from the deep mire here,
Don't let me drown in this swallowing fear.
Save me, O LORD, from my family of hate,
From sweeping waters, and pits in their wake.

Answer me, LORD, from Your goodness in love;
In Your great mercy see I've had enough!
Where is Your face? See Your servant in pain?
Answer me quickly, or all is in vain.

Come near, deliver me from wicked foes;
You know I'm used in their pleasures below;
See how the rebels are gathered against You?
Their scorn is piercing my heart through and through.

I looked for sympathy, yet there was none,
I looked for comfort, and found here no-one.
They served me bile when I dined on my food,
They served me vinegar in my thirst.

May these same woes on their table be set
With their own snares and becoming their net.
In retribution, oh, make their sight dimmer,
May their far reaches be broken, condemned.

Pour out Your fury, LORD, let them see wrath.
Take them in quickly for this aftermath.
May love desert them where they stake their tents;
Let no one enter, let none be their friend.

They persecuted the servants with pains,
gossiped of shame over those You detained.
Charge them with crime upon crime, this is justice;
Do not extend mercy to the corrupt.

May they be blotted from Your book of life,
Banned from the list of the righteous who rise.
But as for me, now afflicted with pain,
Praying salvation, oh God, be ordained.

Then, I will praise the sure name of my God,

Loudly applaud Him with thanksgiving songs.

This praise will please my LORD more than the oxen,

More than a bull with its horns and fetlocks.

Yes, then the poor will come see and be glad!

May every seeker find His habitat!

Indeed, the LORD hears Your isolate pleas;

He never abandons His captives or leaves.

Heaven and earth, oh, let all praise The LORD!

All swimming things in the seas prove His Word!

Zion will praise Him Who rescues His own.

And, in His delight, they rebuild Zion's zones.

He rebuilds Judah, and people will come,

Settling in it, possessing as one;

Children of servants of God will inherit,

And all who love our LORD's name in their midst.

PSALM 70

(For the director of music. Of David. A petition)
Tune: ROCK OF AGES CLEFT FOR ME
"Toplady," Thomas Hastings (1830)
Alternate tunes:
"Cuyler," J. Hyatt Brewer (1905)
"Redhead," Richard Redhead (1853)

Hurry God, oh, save the day!
　　Quicken steps to help, I pray.
May the pirates of my life
　　Come to spar a harsh demise,
Be together put to shame;
When You stir them to disgrace.

May the ones who said to me,
　　"Ha! A-ha!" earn grief on grief.
But may those who seek Your mind
　　Find their gladness by Your side;
And may those who long for God,
Find Your saving grace for all.

Hear them saying, "God is great!"

 Always hear, "The LORD is great!"

As for me, I languish more

 Poor and needy for the LORD.

Come be quick, O LORD, I pray!

Come deliver; don't delay!

PSALM 71

Tune: I AM THINE OH LORD (DRAW ME NEARER)
W. Howard Doane (1875)

I take my place, LORD, in Your hand;

Your refuge, safe, I claim.

Never let me, LORD,

Be put to shame here in Your righteous home.

    Oh, listen! Turn Your ear my way!

    Will You save and rescue me?

    Come and be my home and cornerstone,

    Be the One to which I go.

Salvation comes by Your command,

My Fortress all secure!

Deliver me, from the cruel hands,

Let my honor be assured.

    For You are all my Sovereign Hope,

    My confidence since youth.

    From my birth I've rested in Your arms;

    When You brought me from the womb.

And, forever I will extol You, LORD;

I'm a symbol now to the crowd;

Your strong tower is true for me

Your praise is in my mouth!

    I declare Your splendor all day long.

    Do not leave me when I'm old;

    Do not oust me when my strength is gone.

    For my enemies are bold.

Those who lay in wait, conspiring,

Saying, "God forsakes His own;

Let's seek him out and we'll take him down,

For none will rescue now."

    I am old, LORD! Do not wander far!

    My God, come quick to save!

    May accusers perish in their shame;

    May their wishes be disgraced.

As for me, I hope and will always hope;

I will praise You more and more.

My mouth will tell of Your righteous deeds,

Of Your saving wondrous power.

How can I tell all that You have done?

But, I will proclaim Your might;

All day long I praise the One Who saves.

You're the Sovereign LORD, alone!

I will proclaim Your righteous deeds,

They belong to You alone.

In my younger days, You taught the way,

now my heart is full of song.

All will marvel, even when I'm gray!

Do not leave me in this hour!

I long to shout Your righteous power

To the generations now.

Your mighty acts should be told to all
Who are coming into the world.
When I speak of You, Your great commands,
And Your deeds, the skies confer!

> Who is like You, Faithful LORD?
> Though You brought me troubled times,
> Many bitter tears in awful strife,
> Will You now restore my life?

I have sunk to depths in the cold, hard earth;
Still, you will revive my soul.
You will comfort me and bring me hope;
Once more, I will be whole.

> I will praise You with a singing harp
> For Your truth and faithfulness;
> I will play my praise in chords and strings,
> Holy One of Israel's strength!

My lips will shout for joy and praise
When I sing of all You have done.
For I am the one You helped and raised,
So I'll praise You all day long!
    Telling every child who will hear
    Of Your acts, which I esteem.
    I will mention those who sought my life
    For You put them all to shame.

PSALM 72

(Solomon's Prayer, a Royal Psalm of Blessing)
Tune: COME THOU FOUNT OF EVERY BLESSING
"Nettleton," John Wyeth (1813)

Now endow the King with justice,

Wisened justice, only God.

Now endow the Royal Son with

Holy righteousness to judge.

May He rule Your people fairly

With the faithfulness of truth!

Rule upright for the afflicted,

In Your justice He is good.

May Your mountains make the people

Prosper through Your corridors;

May the hills bring righteous fruits and

May the King defend the poor.

For the bitter and afflicted,

Pray their young ones' needs be borne.

Save the children of the needy;

May He stop the burdensome.

May the King endure forever,
Ever as the shining sun,
Everlasting as our moon glows
Throughout generations.
May the royal Son refresh us
Showers cadence from above
On a field mown, due for water,
Like the rain will nurture earth.

In His day, may all the righteous
Flourish with prosperity!
May this wealth, abounding goodness,
Like the moon's recurrence keep.
May He rule from every ocean
And from rivers to their lands
May the ends of all the earth bow,
Desert tribes bow to His hand.

May the hostile armies lick the

Dust from where He stood them up.

May the kings of Tarshish markets'

Distant shores bring kingly goods.

May the double kings of Sheba

And of Seba bring their gifts.

To the King, may all the kings bow

Serving His good providence.

For the King will absolutely

Save the needy who cry out.

The afflicted, who have no one,

He will help to make a route.

He will see them in His pity,

See the sick and weakly needs,

He will save the ones in sorrow

Weeping violence of their graves.

He will rescue from oppression,

they are precious in His sight.

May He live long, may He prosper!

Sheba's gold shall make Him bright.

May His people pray forever

for His blessedness all day.

May the grain abounding always

in the land and hilltops sway.

May the crops become like Lebanon

thriving like the grassy fields.

May His name endure forever;

likened to the sun's own yields.

Then all nations will find blessings

through the royal Son and King.

They will call Him blessed LORD God,

They will praise the King of Kings.

Praise the God of Israel, Praise Him!~
Who does marvels with acclaim!
He alone is worth all blessing,
Praises to His glorious name!
Now the final word of David
Son of Jesse here proclaims:
May the whole of earth forever,
filled with glory, bless His name.

Tag: Amen and Amen.

CAPTUREMEBOOKS

THE TEN COMMANDMENTS

Exodus 20 (NIV)

And God spoke all these words:

[2] "I am the LORD your God, who brought you out of Egypt, out of the land of slavery.

[3] "You shall have no other gods besides me.

[4] "You shall not make for yourself an image in the form of anything in heaven above or on the earth beneath or in the waters below. [5] You shall not bow down to them or worship them; for I, the LORD your God, am a jealous God, punishing the children for the sin of the parents to the third and fourth generation of those who hate me, [6] but showing love to a thousand generations of those who love me and keep my commandments.

[7] "You shall not misuse the name of the LORD your God, for the LORD will not hold anyone guiltless who misuses His name.

[8] "Remember the Sabbath day by keeping it holy. [9] Six days you shall labor and do all your work, [10] but the seventh day is a sabbath to the LORD your God. On it you shall not do any work, neither you, nor your son or daughter, nor your male or female servant, nor your animals, nor any foreigner residing in your towns. [11] For in six days the LORD made the heavens and the earth, the sea, and all that is in them, but He rested on the seventh day. Therefore the LORD blessed the Sabbath day and made it holy.

[12] "Honor your father and your mother, so that you may live long in the land the LORD your God is giving you.

[13] "You shall not murder.

[14] "You shall not commit adultery.

[15] "You shall not steal.

[16] "You shall not give false testimony against your neighbor.

[17] "You shall not covet your neighbor's house. You shall not covet your neighbor's wife, or his male or female servant, his ox or donkey, or anything that belongs to your neighbor."

THE AUTHOR

As a young adult during the Jesus music era of the '70s, all but one of the enclosed hymn tunes was sung in my local church. At 17, when I moved to attend Bible College in Montana, the students all seemed to be singing contemporary Christian music in gatherings with their guitars, and they were preferring their new music to their classical arts education, much to the college professors' chagrin. Educators, inspite of the students' insistence that church music was in the throes of a great transformation, persisted in training their students for jobs in classical arenas and traditional churches, and this course of study eventually provided me with a double degree in Bible and church music. (B.A.)

After graduations, while I was away in Africa, America's Contemporary Christian Music morphed into a full-blown Western genre called, "Contemporary Christian Worship," and church bands grew up as electronic keyboards and digital computers became accessible to the public. This technology brought about the forecasted significant transition to Church music, while it also served to settle me into a surreal no-man's land between digital pop and textbook hymns.

A legal education followed toward a more pragmatic career, one in which a living might be made, but a funny thing began happening in my understanding of scripture. My eyes were opened to theories of God's law as the things I was taught in American law began to emerge in my scripture reading. Much to my disbelief, I began to see that God brought justice and mercy to nations who followed the Hebrew's Ten Commandments as the basis for modern law. There is a marked difference in the welfare of the people when a nation rejects these fundamentals. It became clear to me through reading the prophets and the New Testament that the Kingdom of God was made from the lawful descendants of Abraham, Isaac and Jacob and the Liberating King by whom all believers are lawfully adopted into the family of God, grafted into the vine (linage of Jesus, through His blood and he seal of the Holy Spirit).

The Psalms seemed full of legal theories of right, wrong and equitable blessings, justice and judgment. These personal expressions of worship contain the full range of history, testimonies, and important spiritual teaching on the priority of Lordship, and loving the Kingdom. Singing or reciting the Psalms in context is a teaser to spiritual depth like working a crossword puzzle is to the mind.

It is my prayer that singing, reciting the testimonies and laments, and performing the Psalms helps bring about a revival of communal faith in the LORD. May we act as a connected body of Christ without broken links, as neighbors, in unity of purpose. May we minister to each other including psalm-singing, as pleases the LORD. This book is meant to enrich congregational worship and to serve individual needs.

The best way to thank an author is to write a review.

Please feel free to connect with us on Facebook @ Psalm-Hymns   Singable Psalms
Or order other products:
www.CaptureBookstore.com

CPSIA information can be obtained
at www.ICGtesting.com
Printed in the USA
BVHW040026160521
607271BV00013B/72